Shattered by Shame... Crowned in Glory

Laurie Smucker

CREATION
HOUSE
PRESS

Library of Congress Control Number: 2002105471
International Standard Book Number: 0-88419-926-6

Published in the United States of America
02 03 04 05 06 07   9 8 7 6 5 4 3 2 1

To contact the author:

Write: Laurie Smucker
       Crowned in Glory Ministries
       Christ's Center Church
       530 West 7th
       Junction City, Oregon 97448

E-mail: crownedinglory@juno.com

Phone: (541) 998-3015

DEDICATION

This book is dedicated to persons of different generations, different ethnic backgrounds and different walks of life. You may be young or old, black or white, rich or poor. Somewhere, someone or some circumstance caused you to become stuck in the grip of shame. As you read in this book the life-changing principles from God's Word, may you begin to exchange the shame from your own shattered life and be crowned in God's magnificent glory.

In loving memory of:

My dad, who went to be with Jesus on February 3, 1988.

And my sweet niece, Cassidy, who also went on before us on December 26, 1995.

ACKNOWLEDGMENTS

My deepest appreciation to:

My dearest friend and husband, Mark. For the last twenty years you have stood by my side like a rock, always faithful and consistent as God transformed my shattered life and crowned me with His amazing glory. I am forever grateful to God for giving me more than I could ever hope for in a husband. I love you, and I cherish our lives together.

Our three priceless children, Aaron, Stefanie and Adam. You three are a "crown of glory" to me and your dad. Each of you bring tremendous joy into our lives. God has given you to us as "triple portions." We love you deeply and admire your personalities, gifts and talents. May you grow up to be stronger and more courageous in your walk with Jesus than either of your parents.

My parents. Thank you for the gift of my life. The shame we've experienced led us to repentance, and in exchange we received the greatest gift of all, our salvation. Now we are free to continually change from glory to glory. Thank you for letting me write our story so that others can be completely set free from the bondage of shame. I love you dearly.

My family. We have all felt shame at one time or another in our lives. None of our shame is the same, but it's how we exchange our shame for His glory that counts.

May you see me in a different light for the first time, broken and more desperate for Jesus than I've ever been before. I love you with all my heart.

My pastor, Jon Bowers, and his sweet wife, Lynna Gay, who have stood with me for twenty life-changing years. Thank you for seeing a "diamond in the rough" when I walked through the doors of Christ's Center Church at age twenty. Thank you for believing in me and for never giving up on me. You have truly been an amazing example of the love of Jesus. I cherish our friendship.

My church family at Christ's Center Church. There are truly too many names to mention or else I would fill an entire chapter. Thank you for standing beside me and helping me to walk out of shame into God's glory. I am forever thankful. May God richly bless your lives for laying them down for mine.

My dearest friends with whom I have shared my deepest shame. Only God knows what those long coffee breaks and lunch dates did in my life. I was able to reveal my hidden shame to you, bringing it into the light, so God could shine his love on it. These times have been so precious to me. I can only cry in private when I think of what we've shared. "Thank you" can never be enough. I love you.

Sandi Tompkins, my editor, mentor and now lifelong friend. You have masterfully helped bring my writing to a work of excellence. I can say that to you because you're the only one who really knows how far I have come. I can only hope and pray that we'll be writing together again soon.

Dr. Allen Quain and the staff at Creation House Press. Thank you for embracing my story and causing my dream of publication to come true. You have been so professional to work with, and I appreciate all you have done to make this book a work of art. Blessings to all of you.

My precious friend and artist. Thank you for capturing me on the front cover of this book, as only God sees me, "Crowned in Glory."

Most importantly, my precious Lord and Savior, Jesus. Words cannot be formed to express my love for You. I am that woman who is pouring her shame over Your feet and anointing them with her tears. Thank You for lifting me out of my shattered life and crowning me with Your amazing glory.

FOREWORD

The Exchange...

The Book of Isaiah speaks of an exchange that takes place when we decide by faith to receive the gracious gift of God's salvation. This exchange is the reason men and woman for two millennia have exuberantly declared their receipt of this gift by accepting the gospel. One of the greatest transfers in the moment of salvation is the abolishment of shame in exchange for a life of destiny and hope.

Shame is one the most powerful means by which darkness takes hold on a life and slowly eliminates the possibility of a future filled with blessing. I am grateful for this book by Laurie Smucker—yet another awesome story of a life impacted by deliverance from shame. My prayer is that many will read it and experience firsthand a destiny free of shame, either by God's elimination of it through salvation or a renewed sense of taking hold of their rights through the salvation they have already received.

The testimony you will read in this book reminds me that I am one of those grateful ones who is now rejoicing in the blessings I've experienced in knowing Jesus! During one very difficult time for me a few years ago, I took some time away from ministry for the purpose of focusing on several deep issues that had surfaced in my life. It was a very hard time for my family and me, yet

God was faithful. He placed some amazing encouragers around us who helped us through what became a pivotal time for us. Many special people were in our lives at that time; two of them were Laurie and her husband, Mark. I was impressed with their calm graciousness and complete confidence in God's ability to make right all the issues. That was what I needed to hear. I now know the source of the strength and grace in Laurie's life; she was simply giving out of the rich fountain she had discovered in her own times of distress. She had made an exchange of her shame and had accepted her destiny in God.

I have said many times since then, "If only people could see how the body of Christ responded to the diffi-culties in my life." I never felt the spirit of judgmentalism and condemnation that so many attribute to Christians these days. I saw in Mark and Laurie the attitude that I know every human being wants to experience when walking through a hard place. Truly, Jesus has the answers for any problems mankind has to confront, and we have it in the exchange He offers us in His awesome salvation.

It is an honor to be asked to write this foreword for Laurie. She and Mark have displayed such amazing sta-bility and encouragement in their ministry to others. I became acquainted with their extended family when I met Mark's mother, LeeAnn Smucker, during the time of her Crossroads Discipleship Training School at the University of the Nations in Hawaii. I was impressed by LeeAnn's courage and love for God, and I found in her the very same love for God's mercy and grace that so punctuates the lives and ministry of Mark and Laurie. As I learned the story of LeeAnn's loss of her husband, I was immediately drawn in compassion toward her family. Not long thereafter, I met Mark and several of his ministry associates and arranged to take part in a time of worship at their fellowship.

My first impression of Laurie made me feel as though I was the one being ministered to even though I had been invited to share at their church. Clearly her heart was to serve and not to be served. For ten years, I have been able to work alongside the Smuckers, and each year their commitment to impart courage, blessing and grace just seems to grow.

Laurie Smucker has exchanged her sorrow and shame for Christ's joy and hope in her life, and she is now a vessel for His glory. As you read her story, may you be motivated to let go of your shame and receive God's enabling grace.

—Bob Fitts
WORSHIP LEADER AND INTEGRITY MUSIC SONGWRITER

CONTENTS

Introduction xv

1 Roots of Shame 1

2 The Power of His Love Brings Healing . . .17

3 The Power of His Grace Produces Faith . .33

4 Father to the Fatherless 45

5 His Eye Is on the Sparrow 61

6 Unshakable Kingdom 81

7 The Power of His Glory Breaks Shame . .101

8 A New Name: World-Changers 123

9 Touching Hearts, Changing Lives 149

10 Wash Over Me 173

11 Pressing On .193

12 Send Revival .213

Epilogue .229

INTRODUCTION

This personal account of my life is a journey that has taken me through shame, dishonor and injustice into the great adventure of life: serving Jesus, the King of kings and Lord of lords.

Over the years, I have exchanged my shame for His glory, my dishonor for His honor, my injustice for His justice. I traded my lonely, empty past for a glorious future.

Where I was disgraced, Jesus poured out His healing grace upon my life. To the areas in my life where I have felt brokenhearted, Jesus has brought healing.

My disobedience has been traded for obedience, my pride for humility. I've exchanged bondage in my life for the freedom we receive when Jesus is Lord of our lives. I've traded hate, anger, fear and abandonment for the perfect, unfailing love of my Savior.

In my life shame exchanges continue to happen again and again. I pray that, through my story, you will experience the power of the Holy Spirit touching your life as you exchange your own shame for something greater.

God's exchange rate is better than anything this world has to offer, and rest assured, we will receive a greater return on our investment. The more we give to Jesus, making Him Lord of everything in our lives, the more He can pour into us. If our lives are full of ourselves, we can never experience freedom. We must pour ourselves out completely so Jesus can pour His life into ours. He is looking for empty, broken vessels to house His glory. We must make the kinds of exchanges needed to change our destiny.

My prayer is that this book will help to release each of us from the bondage of shame and to exchange it for the glory of the Lord.

I would like to define shame before we begin. I am not a psychologist, professional counselor or pastor. The only creditable definition of shame I can offer is through personal experience, study and revelation through the Holy Spirit. I also would like to honor Craig Hill, whose teaching tapes on *Identifying Shame* brought much revelation to me.[1]

Shame creates a feeling that something must be wrong with us. Shame causes a sinking feeling rooted in fear. Shame causes us to hate ourselves and to feel unclean. Shame makes us feel that no matter what we do, it will never be good enough.

Shame started in the Garden of Eden. Adam and Eve's disobedience led them to sin. As a result, they instantly recognized their nakedness and felt shame. They covered their naked bodies and tried to hide from God. Adam and Eve were afraid to show themselves because sin had broken their fellowship with God.

The effects of sin spread rapidly. Eve involved Adam in her disobedience, then blamed the serpent. Adam blamed God first (for creating the woman), then he blamed Eve. They were trying to excuse their sin and cover up their shame.

As with Adam and Eve, shame causes us to blame

others for our past and all the injustice that has happened to us. Injustice happens because we live in a fallen world full of people who sin, who have been shamed and who walk in selfishness.

Sin and shame were not in God's original plan. Sin, shame and, eventually, death entered our world because of disobedience in the Garden of Eden. God's plan was a beautiful paradise where we could take refuge, an oasis, a sanctuary to enjoy the very breath of God in the early morning breeze.

Shame occurs in our lives when something shakes our world. It can happen after divorce, death, or verbal, physical or sexual abuse. Shame usually occurs through the people we love most.

Shame can happen when we or other people make wrong choices. Shame carries over from our past. Our wounds and disappointments come from a time when our needs were not met. Shamed adults shame others, such as parents who shame their children. This promotes feelings of worthlessness that grow in our hearts and cause us to feel that we have no value.

Shame can even come through churches. People shame other people. People caught in sin are shamed verbally as well as physically through how we respond to them. We need to learn how to deal with sin without shaming people. We should "love the sinner but hate the sin."

Shame compels us to form compulsive habits, such as smoking, drinking, overeating, and fulfilling fleshly and sexual desires. Our flesh craves satisfaction. Shame rises up to torment each of us. The enemy feeds on our thoughts of our past activities. He will convince us that if we would just do this, we would feel better. This feeling of satisfaction lasts only for a moment, then we experience both shame and guilt. The feeling comes over us that we are worthless because we did the wrong thing—again.

Shame comes from Satan, not from God. It leaves us with a bad feeling that we will never be able to overcome it. We feel so ashamed that we must hide it from people and then from God. We try to make everything on the outside look good, even if everything on the inside is breaking apart.

Conviction comes from God whenever our actions or choices are wrong. We can receive freedom from guilt by repenting of our sins, our wrong attitudes and actions.

Even more unfortunately, shame grows like weeds in a flower bed or garden. If you don't get the roots, the weeds keep coming back and will take over the flower garden, leaving results that are devastating to the human eye. Weeds choke out the flowers and the plants so they will not produce a harvest.

Just the same, shame, if left in our lives for a long time, will choke out all the beauty and ultimately destroy all the fruit in our lives.

When we allow Jesus to be Lord of every area of our lives, we can become like a beautiful garden. When we reflect the image of God, we draw attention wherever we go. We have been set apart, and we should look different from people who have not surrendered their shame to the Lord.

When deep conviction comes to our spirit, we know when we have stepped over the line. That's when it's time to humble ourselves and repent of our sins.

As we cry out in repentance, the guilt is wiped away

because of the shed blood of Jesus. If we were to write our sins on a blackboard and then cry out in repentance, Jesus would take an eraser and wipe our guilt away forever. He would remember our sins no more.

When Jesus went to the cross, He bore all our sin and shame. It was enough. We can be forgiven because the blood of Jesus was shed on the cross and because of the power of His resurrection.

I believe shame is Satan's biggest tool to keep each of us from fulfilling our destiny. If the enemy can do this, he can rob us from being effective in our personal lives and keep us from being all that God created us to be.

How can you know if you walk in shame? Here is a test you can take to determine the answer. If one or more of these statements apply to you, you can be assured you do.

1. You must remain in control of your feelings. Crying and laughing must be kept under control. Some of you will not experience feelings or emotions because you have stuffed them for so long. You are reserved and aloof.

2. You can never admit when you are wrong or if you have made a mistake. You have a need to do everything right. You must be perfect and look perfect. In a public place, your appearance must be perfect.

3. When things are beyond your control, you blame others or yourself. You feel angry. This results in yelling or punishing.

4. You deny anything that is going on inside

your heart; you have no feelings at all. You shut down and do not express joy or sorrow. You are afraid to have an opinion and will not be perceptive.

5. You do not have needs and will not ask for a favor from anyone, as you do not want to put people out. You are self-sufficient and cannot receive from others.

6. You try hard to keep everything a secret. You try to hide things. You must be tough, and so it is never okay to release anything.

7 You will not open up your heart to anyone. You do not trust anyone because relationships are unreliable and unpredictable.

8. You cannot say no. You will not try new things because it would be out of your control or comfort zone. You try to make everyone happy.

9. You experience emotions of anger and rage.

10. You have a feeling deep inside that if you do not succeed, you will not be loved.

If you are walking in shame, it is my prayer that the Holy Spirit will use this book to breathe life into all your areas of shame. But you must be open to letting God transform your life and propel each area of shame into a freedom you have never felt before.

Jesus longs to set each of us free from every broken or hurting area in our lives, to give beauty for ashes, joy instead of mourning, the garment of praise for the spirit of heaviness.

Jesus wants to rebuild our lives so we will rise up and come to life. He wants to give us a future and a hope. But it is our job to seek Him so He can be found.

I want to encourage you to make your own shame exchanges with the Lord. Not one of us is alike, and none of our shame is the same. God has a special individual encounter and a glorious future waiting for each of us as we exchange the old for the new, leave our past behind and press forward to being all that God has called us to be.

ONE

Roots of Shame

I felt like dancing with glee as my dad came in from the damp Oregon weather, bringing in our not-so-perfect eight-foot Douglas fir tree. It seemed absolutely *huge* to my six-year-old eyes. As the branches unfolded, a bad spot in the tree appeared that would need to be hidden. Dad centered the tree between our back picture windows overlooking the valley. As he placed the lighted star on the top of the tree, I would stand back and gaze at it, breathing deeply the sweet pine scent that spread through our home like a whispered message. It said to me, my three brothers and two sisters one joyful, long-awaited word—Christmas.

The youngest of six children, I looked forward to this

holiday more than any other time of year. Thoughts of opening presents, singing Christmas carols, digging in the boxes to find my favorite decorations, and smelling cookies baking had danced in my head for days prior to the tree's grand arrival. Another sweet daydream was our family tearing open all the presents at one time and shouting, "Look what I got! Look what I got!" During these moments, my family seemed like a normal, happy American family. After all, if there is a time for families to be happy, it should be at Christmas.

Dad brought in large barrels of Christmas decorations from the old shed, and we children started pulling out all the bright lights, shiny ornaments and the treasured nativity scene. I loved carefully placing Joseph, Mary, baby Jesus, the three wise men and all the animals on top of Grandma's piano. Then I would sit down and play my childlike version of "Away in the Manger" and "Jingle Bells," among other Christmas carols.

My brother Sam would yell, "Laurie, just knock it off and stop that racket." I would continue playing until he came after me, and then I would run from the room screaming, "Mom, Sam won't let me keep playing the piano! He's going to hurt me!" "I am not," Sam fired back. "You are, too," I'd yell back.

Exasperated, Mom started screaming at both of us, and I felt like sinking into the floor for my part in making her so upset. Great shame began to creep over me. I could never understand what I had done so wrong to get yelled at so often. I wanted to run and hide from all the fighting. Almost every special day of my young life ended in a screaming match of some kind.

By six I'd learned that nearly any situation in our

home could quickly turn into a raging argument. Usually just a few words—a mean joke, a critical comment, a threat or a demand by the older children—would set it off. I tried to cover my ears to keep from hearing the awful, hateful things that my brothers and sisters would yell at one another. Pretty soon Mom or Dad would step in to break it up, but that rarely settled things.

There was always tension mounting in my home, but the fights I hated most were the ones no one could break up—the fights between Mom and Dad.

To me, it seemed as if the tension had been steadily mounting in their lives like steam in a pressure cooker. I remember standing by my mom as she watched the pressure of the steam rise on our old cooker. I'd ask her, "Whatcha doing, Mom?" "Well, Laurie, if you don't watch this needle very carefully, the entire pot could blow up right in our faces." I looked at her strangely and decided I didn't want to be in the kitchen if that thing was going to explode. Then I began to wonder, *How come no one was paying attention to all the outbursts going on around here?* That's how our family life went—one flare-up after another.

Mom and Dad would fight, and I would run out the back door as soon as the screaming started and prayed as hard as I could: "God, please help them stop! Make them stop!" I never stopped to put on shoes or a coat, so within minutes, I'd be shivering, cold and wet. Because my insides hurt so much, I didn't notice it at first. I just kept crying out my childlike pleas to a distant God. One time when I ran out, I stubbed my toe, and it began to bleed. Cautiously I made my way back into the house through the front door to ask for a bandage. Instantly, the fighting stopped, and my bleeding was attended to. This little miracle not only made my toe feel better, but also made me wonder why God couldn't just put a bandage on my family and make it all better, too.

I remember many days filled with Christmas surprises that were crushed by another uproar in our house. We would all go to Christmas Eve service dressed in our new Christmas outfits. I enjoyed the excitement and anticipation I felt sitting through the story of baby Jesus, watching as the last candle on the Advent wreath was lit and then waiting in line for my sack of candy before we left church. Then my dad would drive us through town slowly so we could look at all the Christmas lights. My eyes would twinkle with glee over the excitement of the night, and I'd nudge my dad and ask, "Is it time to go home yet?"

All of us children whined and complained that looking at lights was taking too long and we wanted to go home and open our presents. I think my dad drove even slower until we all were quiet, and then he'd say, "Well, do you think Santa has had time to come?" We'd all scream, "Yes, yes!"

We'd arrive home to a tree surrounded by presents that Santa had brought. I was overwhelmed by all the gifts, but I also felt ashamed because I thought I hadn't been good enough to deserve so much. I questioned myself, *Why would I get everything I wanted and still get yelled at all the time?* This didn't make sense to me. I wanted everyone to be this happy every day of the year. That would have been the greatest Christmas gift I could ever have received: true peace and happiness. But, for the moment, I simply enjoyed the seasonal laughter and joy.

Then reality would come crashing into our lives again because it was time to clean up and go to bed. Of course, no one wanted to help, and it became a major chore to get all six children involved. Jean would say, "Mom, Suzy's not helping." Somehow, Suzy had disappeared and was nowhere to be found. Then the screaming would begin, "Suzy, get in here right this minute! Do you want a spanking?" This would immediately alert me to start picking up faster, because I thought that if I worked harder no one would get yelled at. I'd bring my pile of picked-up wrapping paper to Dad, and he would stuff the paper in our old wood stove. Boy, our house warmed up fast, like the heat that was fanning the flames of everyone's temper.

I waited around, hoping to get thanked for helping, but it never happened. I'd get nervous standing there, so I thought, *Maybe if I did more work, I'd be thanked for being a good girl.* I'd run off and busy myself with bringing dirty dishes to the sink to try and please my mom. In my mind, I felt as if I never pleased anyone. I'd see deep frustration in my mom's eyes, so I'd scurry off to help some more.

When the work was finally done, I'd kiss my parents good night and jump into bed and pray for them. Hundreds of times I prayed, "Please, God, help my parents to stop fighting and help them never to divorce! Amen!" I don't know when I started talking to God, but I thought that only some big powerful God could fix my family's problems.

Eventually, it dawned on me that the only time I felt real peace in our family was after we got to church on Sunday mornings. Of course, getting eight of us ready in only one bathroom made for lots of fights and tension before we ever got out the door. Mom insisted that we all be dressed up in our best Sunday clothes. For me and my sisters, Jean and Suzy, that meant two hours of torture in itchy, frilly, matching dresses that Mom had made. Scrubbed and dressed up as we were, I couldn't help but think that even the nicest clothes couldn't cover up the ugliness hidden under the surface.

During church I sometimes wondered if other people there knew how much fighting went on in our family. *Would anyone want to be friends with us if they knew?* When service started, I tried to sit close to my parents, and Mom would softly rub my ears or play with my hair to keep me still. I loved that feeling, and I would just relax and enjoy the peace I felt with my mom. I tried to listen to what the pastor was saying, but I didn't understand some things. One thing I did know was that it felt comforting to be in church, where people sang together and seemed to treat one another kindly.

Sometimes I found myself staring at other children and wondering what their families were like. *Did they all have fun together like those big families I'd seen on television, or were they screamers like my family?* I couldn't tell from looking at them, but I knew I didn't want them to know about my family. More and more, our fighting became a painful, shameful thing for me. I never really wanted friends to come over because I knew they would ask about all the yelling. Many times I made excuses so no one would come over. Church was good because we all behaved and looked our best. We couldn't fight if we were in church, and that became a place of safety for me.

The only other place I felt safe was on my dad's lap. When he settled into his big easy chair after work, I liked to crawl up, press my ear against his chest and listen to his heart beat. He was always so warm, and he smelled like a

6

sawmill. Other times, I would bring him a glass of iced tea and then watch him read the paper. I desperately wanted to win his affection, and to get his attention, I'd tickle his feet. "You're the ornery one," he'd say, flashing a smile that instantly brightened my mood. He always could make me laugh. I only wished he could do more to hold our family together.

By the time I was ten years old, even these infrequent feelings of safety were crumbling. I found myself yelling like the others and hardening under the strain of daily tension. One thing I noticed about our family fights was that my parents never said they were sorry or asked for forgiveness. In church, the pastor talked about how important forgiveness was for marriages and friendships, but I guess my parents never heard it quite like I did.

I remember my parents trying to be affectionate with one another, but it always seemed forced. I would secretly watch them peck each other three times on the lips before my dad would leave for work. I thought, *They have to love each other, don't they?*

In my mind it looked like they were going through the motions each day, stuck somewhere in their past, where pain and shame must have injured them as children. Our family's wound was deep and oozing, infected with poison. And I realized this germ was spreading to all of us, the next generation. After so many fights and hurts, I wondered how we could possibly forgive enough to cover it all. I became more frightened about what we'd be like in the future. I began to ask myself, *Can I ever change? Can any of us ever change?* Changes were happening, but not the kind I wanted.

As the years went on, my time was filled with going to

school, coming home, eating dinner, helping with chores and then going to bed, only to start the same routine all over again the next day. My Mom had started to work at another sawmill in town when I was five. She worked the night shift most of the time, so we all pitched in and helped with chores.

I remember being paired off with one of my older brothers and doing the dishes every third night. With a family of six children, there are lots of dirty dishes after a meal. Joe would wash, and I would dry. If the dishes weren't clean enough, they went back in the dirty pile. This always caused a rift between the person washing and drying. "Dad," I yelled, "Joe isn't getting the dishes clean enough to dry them." Dad would come in. "Joe, what's all the fuss about? Start over on these dishes and do it right this time." Then he would look and me and say firmly, "Laurie, quit being so picky! Just be quiet and do your job right." Most of the time, Joe wouldn't say a word. He would just look away and keep washing the dishes. I always felt ashamed of myself after I had told on one of my siblings. I never wanted anyone to get yelled at anymore than they had to, especially Joe.

There was fighting by our family almost every day. There were seldom any words of encouragement in our family, and I felt as if I was never good enough. For a young girl, that was hard to handle.

As I began my high school years, most of my older siblings had graduated and moved out of the house. They all seemed to have gotten on with their lives, and I only saw them on special holidays such as Thanksgiving and Christmas. My sister Suzy and I were the only two left at home, so the noise level went down several notches. No longer did I have to share a room with anyone. It felt good to have some space. My sister and I had our differences, of course. But I stayed out of her way, and she stayed out of mine. We fought occasionally, but these screaming matches seemed quite minor compared to those in my family's past.

At this stage in my life, I felt insecure as many teenagers do. So much importance was placed on being popular and excelling in everything. I remember trying out for volleyball and going to practice twice a day. I remember becoming aware of my physical body and wanting to be thin. I decided to stop eating, except for one meal a day. It felt good to be in control of *something* when my family's life felt so out of control. I felt safe keeping busy with sports and having fun with my friends. Oftentimes, I'd ride my bike over to a friend's house to spend the day. We would put on some old fifties tunes, sing and dance, laugh and have fun. I was too ashamed to tell my friends what was going on in my home, so I learned to escape the pain by being silly and making others laugh. This was my only way to cut loose and relieve the stress in my life. Many times the tension I experienced felt like a balloon blown up too tight, ready to pop. I knew I should tell someone how I was feeling, but I couldn't get up the nerve to trust anyone.

I was only fourteen at the time, with so much future ahead of me. So much promise. So much hope. I continued to pray, "God, please hold my family together. Please help us to make it just a little while longer."

As our family was shrinking in size, the problems were mounting. I remember going on a summer vacation to *Disneyland with the hopes that this would be a turning point for my family. Disneyland was the happiest place in the world, right? Surely, going to a fun place couldn't hurt; it could only help.* Mom seemed sad and distant, so I tried to make the most of it and have as much fun as I could. My sister seemed reserved, but sometimes she would let her hair down and have some fun, too. My Dad and I rode all the rides and laughed our heads off. I thought, *Maybe, if we could have more fun, everyone would be happy.* I tried to escape the pain by dreaming up a fantasy family.

I remember late one night that winter, my parents got in a fight, and my sister came crying for my help. Desperately, she begged me to go into the kitchen and stop the fighting. Somehow she thought I could fix it. I ran into the dining room to find out what all the yelling was about. Mom sat at the dining room table crying, her hand on the side of her head as she leaned her elbow on the table. She looked up at me with tear-filled eyes and said she wanted a divorce. I couldn't believe what I was hearing. I wanted to hold my hands over my ears to keep them from hearing those burning words. I had prayed against this for years. *This couldn't be coming true, I screamed inside my head.* My heart pounded wildly, and my thoughts scattered in every direction. I couldn't think straight, and I didn't know what to do.

Dad made the next move. I had never seen him so angry in all my life. He announced he was going for a walk, and when he got back, she better have made up her mind. As I watched my dad leave, I felt raw fear clutch my throat. *Now, what would we do and with whom would I live?* I glanced over at my mom, who looked pathetic. Immediately, my emotions began to take over. I felt a combination of deep sadness and raging anger. I ran off to my room and threw myself onto the bed, burying my head under the covers. As I turned my head to face the wall, I thought, *Maybe if I go to sleep, I'll wake up and this will all be a bad dream.* I tossed and turned all night in a fitful sleep.

My parents were giving up. The reality of divorce came crashing down on my heart. The pain hurt so bad I thought my heart might break. Lurking in the dark shadows were my parents' hidden lifestyles of sin that none of us yet knew about. I could almost hear Satan and his cohorts laughing with delight as they nailed the coffin shut on the life of my family. I felt empty, lifeless, deserted and helpless. My sense of home life was destroyed. "Who will stop the bleeding now?" I screamed at God. "Where are you now, God, when I need that bandage?"

I was broken and crushed by my parents' choices. *Did they think about how I might feel about all of this? Did they even care?* I wondered. I raised my fist to God, who I felt had failed me miserably, and yelled, "If this is the way You play, God, I'm not going to have anything to do with You." That night I made a vow that I would never cry again.

The next morning, while my dad was away at work, my mom sat my sister and I down at the dining room table. I felt a wall of self-protection go up around me as she spoke: "Suzy and Laurie, I want you to know that I have found another man. What do you think? If I can get the house, will you live with me?"

My eyes almost popped out of my head, I was so angry. "Mom, I would never live with you," I said coldly, shoving my chair out of the way. I picked up my bag, looked at my older sister and waited for her response. "I won't live with you, either," she said. With a sigh of relief, I ran out the door to catch the bus. I remember being angry and cold. My head was reeling with confusion. I felt betrayed at the deepest level of my emotions. I had never felt such searing pain penetrating my heart.

I vividly remember slamming my locker door at school, and one of my friends asked me what was wrong. I don't remember if I told anyone that day. I was mad at the world, so I replied, "Just get out of my way and leave me alone." I was so enraged that I wanted to punch someone. My emotions were so raw and filled with hatred and malice, they could unleash on anybody who looked at me wrong. "How am I to cope, God?" I cried out. "Who will help me now? Where are You, God?"

The weeks leading up to Christmas were a blur to me. My sister and I both shut down in our own ways. I became tough with an "I can make it all by myself" attitude. My sister gave up trying altogether. She probably thought, *Why bother with anything anymore? It doesn't really matter.*

My parents continued living under the same roof. It felt like we were living in a house that soon would wear a sign saying, "This family has vacated the premises." We ate and slept there in the midst of a cold war no one was going to win.

A couple of weeks later, my dad fell from a ladder at work and shattered his knee cap. More hopelessness crept into my heart. Now my dad couldn't even rescue me. *Who will take care of me? Did anyone care?*

Dad needed surgery to put pins and screws into place. He came home a few days later. He wore a cast from his ankle to his hip and occupied a hospital bed in the living room.

Now, home felt like death. Nothing was really living.

It felt like this sick virus overflowed into our broken hearts. I could feel my dad's anger and grief over his failed marriage. Every time my mom would bring something for him to eat or drink, Dad would unleash snide remarks at her: "So, are you feeling guilty today? Is that why you decided to take care of me like a wife should?" To my surprise, Mom never responded to those gibes.

That year, not even Christmas could save us from sorrow. Christmas came and went with little to be happy about. We no longer went to church, so I couldn't escape from the hell at home. I went into a survival mode. I thought, *If I can just stay out of the house and keep my mind occupied, then I won't have to face anyone or anything. It worked for a while.*

One day, Dad gave me money to go grocery shopping with a friend's mom. She showed me how to buy groceries. I remember standing in the meat section, my eyes glazing over, trying to decide what to buy and wondering what I would do with it after I bought it. *So this was the way it was going to be*, I thought to myself. I tried to tell myself, *It's not that bad. I can do this.* I felt fearful and overwhelmed. *How was I to know what to shop for, let alone how to cook it? Did moms just know what to buy? Or did someone teach them?*

When we returned home, Mom was packing her car to leave. I couldn't believe what I was seeing. I was shocked. I thought, *Was this planned? Did Dad get me out of the house so I wouldn't be here when she left?* Those few moments were a blur to me. I looked over at my friend's mom as if to ask her what I should do. She invited me to come over to her house. I said, "All right, I'll come." I desperately wanted to be rescued. Here was my way out, and I didn't have to face my mom and say good-bye. I didn't want to say good-bye because I didn't want her to go. I still hoped things would turn around and that my family life could be restored. As we threw the grocery bags on the table, I secretly hoped my mom would come out of her bedroom, but she never did. As I climbed back into my friend's car, I wanted to run back and beg my mom not to go. I don't know what stopped me—pride, anger or fear of rejection. I just went home with my friend's mom and ran away from all the pain and great shame I was feeling. I remember thinking, *I need to get out of here. I need to run away.* At that moment, I decided I would never speak to my mom again. If she were going to leave me for another man, then she could not be my mom. These were the feelings Satan was placing in my heart at this time. Of course, my mom loved me, but she was living in her own world of pain and shame.

During the next few weeks I had to learn to drive. I was only fourteen, and yet someone had to get to the grocery store to buy food. My Dad was still in a cast. It was hysterical watching him try to get into the pickup truck with his cast. We had to find something to laugh at, or life would bring us down. My older sister seemed afraid to drive. Sometimes I would get frustrated with how she was dealing with things. But all six of us children seemed to be in our private world of hurt. We really didn't have the tools to help one another through any of this, so we simply ignored one another for the most part.

Life went on, but there was a noticeable change in our house. All the yelling seemed to have left. No more marriage, no more fighting. I think that's when I took on the responsibility of trying to keep my dad happy. I rationalized, *If I do everything just right, then there will be no more yelling in this house.*

I began to fill a void at home that a young teenager should never have to fill. I couldn't cook very well, but I could clean and do laundry. My Dad and I ate simple meals: macaroni and cheese, Hamburger Helper and lots of junk food. I remember making cookies one day. I didn't put everything away right after I used it. My Dad got so upset with me over something that seemed so small. I felt hopeless. I wanted to scream, *Why should I do anything around here anymore?* But instead, I cleaned up the mess and kept trying to make him happy. I held in a lot of the pressure of trying to be perfect. I kept telling myself, *I can handle this. I'll be all right.* Little did I know, I had my own pressure cooker steaming out of control.

My daily life consisted of going to school, playing sports, coming back home and trying to play the part of the woman of the house. School and sports became my first avenues of escape. I threw myself into being the best I could be.

As the days went by, I became increasingly hostile toward my mom and dad. Many times my dad would leave on weekends, and my sister and I were left at home or at a friend's house. It was then that I began to feel deserted and lonely enough to drink. I was trying to bury the pain of shame by getting drunk. I was still just fourteen, but I justified my actions: *How else could I deal with this hurt and anger raging in my heart and mind? Did my parents expect I could handle all this? Who was helping me with all my pain? No one!*

I was unable to forgive, and bitterness found its way into my heart. The party lifestyle was inviting because it deadened my pain. I remember waiting at a convenience store, hoping I could talk someone into buying me some beer. I felt sneaky and powerful after I had accomplished my mission. Drinking gave me a false sense of enjoyment and covered up the pain of shame for hours. The next morning I would wake up and try to get out of bed, but by then my head throbbed and my stomach was so queasy that I thought I might throw up if I moved.

I realized then that drinking would not mask the heaviness and hopelessness tugging at my heart. An intense guilt and shame continued to invade my life. Nothing seemed to erase the deep emptiness and loneliness I felt in the pit of my stomach. I was spiraling out of control, losing my grip. *Who could help me?*

[1] You can order these tapes at P.O. Box 320, Littleton, Colorado 80120, or by calling 303-797-1139.

TWO

The Power of His Love Brings Healing

The help I so desperately needed was not coming from anywhere. *Shame…would I ever be free from this torment of shame I felt was overtaking my life?*

After my parents' divorce, I made a vow that I would somehow succeed and be someone despite my parents failing me. I would be perfect at everything I did. I would work hard and make something of my life, so everyone had better get out of my way. But I had not found happiness…not yet. My life was full of self and empty of love. More than a year had gone by since I'd heard the words "I love you" from anyone.

However, my loveless life began to change before my fifteenth birthday, thanks to my two best friends, Colleen and Tammy. They gave me a heart necklace. They told me how much they loved me and how much they were concerned that I was destroying my life. We sat in a grocery store parking lot, and they pleaded with me to stop partying. At that moment, their love caused me to cry for the first time in a year. Those tears melted some of the bitterness from my broken heart. I went home with that heart necklace, thinking there must be more to life than what I had been living.

Two weeks later, I was on the road to Nebraska with my aunt and uncle and cousins in their motor home. We were going to a family wedding, and my dad would meet us there. On the way, we stopped to visit family near Spokane, Washington, and we decided to go to church with them the next day.

My heart was soft and tender, ripe for the picking. When I went into that church, I felt the love of Jesus like I had never experienced it before. People were greeting each other with hugs and really loving each other. I couldn't believe what I was seeing. *Could this be what love is all about?* I had to find out. Throughout the church service, I kept listening and watching. When the music played, people enjoyed singing and worshiping Jesus. They talked about Him like they knew Him. I tried to listen to the sermon, but I was too busy experiencing what was going on around me. I felt the genuine love of Jesus for the first time in my life. When the pastor shared the plan of salvation, I found myself raising my hand.

Next I made a move to the front of the church to receive Jesus as Lord of my life. Immediately, my heart felt lighter, and later, I seemed to float out of the church. My life would never be the same again. My destiny was forever changed that day by accepting Jesus as Lord of my life.

I had made my first exchange with God. I gave Him my cold, broken, hardened heart, and He gave me a new heart that was sensitive, free and able to experience love again. (See Ezekiel 11:19.) Through the gift of a heart necklace from my friends, I discovered how hungry I was to be loved, accepted and forgiven. I began to open myself to real love. I had finally met the source of that love: my heavenly Father. If my friends only knew how much that necklace meant to me.

After I made my first exchange, I was given a second gift. I didn't have to do anything to earn it. It was the gift of salvation. I remember sitting on my bed after I got saved and reading Ephesians 2:8 for the first time. As I read the words, "For by grace you have been saved through faith; and that not of yourselves, it is the gift of God" (NAS), I caught my reflection in the mirror. As I gazed at my image, I could see that my appearance was softening. These words of freedom were changing me from the inside out. During those few moments, I felt God's undeserved grace upon my life. A single tear of joy ran down my face.

Although I had been to church many times, I knew there was more to being a Christian than what I'd experienced. I was ready to live for Jesus, but I had no idea what that meant. My aunt, uncle and cousins were a crucial part of that learning process. They gave me a crash course on the Father, Son and Holy Spirit while we were traveling about 2,000 miles in a motor home from Cheney, Washington, to Alliance, Nebraska. I knew I wanted everything Jesus had to offer me. The next step was living this new life out in front of my dad and the rest of my family.

What would they think of the new me? How would they respond? When we begin a new life with Jesus, not everyone accepts the changes that are happening in our heart, soul and mind. I learned quickly that understanding how much Jesus loved me and living it out were two different things. One of the first things Jesus asked me to do was to start showing His love to my dad and mom and to my family and friends. Jesus said in Matthew 22:37–40 to "love the Lord...with all your heart, all your soul, and all your mind" (NLT). Then He said to "love your neighbor as yourself" (NLT). If I was to love others as much as I loved myself, I needed to show that love through my actions, not just with words.

One of the first times I told my dad I loved him was late at night, when I had just gotten home from a basketball game. I remember getting in trouble for being loud after my dad was in bed. I felt frustrated as I wondered how I should respond. In my mind I heard a little voice say, *Tell him you love him.* As I paced back and forth in the hallway, I thought, *Why should I tell him I love him? He was the one yelling at me.* Finally, I said, "Dad, I love you." Dead silence pierced the air at that moment. I waited for his response. I thought, *Is he going to say anything?* After a short time, which felt like forever, he said, "I love you, too. Now go to bed." I nearly jumped for joy when my dad responded. In that moment, love was exchanged between a daughter and her daddy. That love came into my heart from the heavenly Father, and I was able to give that same love away to my earthly dad. The Spirit of God allowed me to glimpse His healing power of love. Our lives were never the same again.

We began to genuinely express love to each other in simple, yet profound, ways. I think I clung to every loving word my dad said. He was devoted to caring for me, and I was devoted to loving him.

Because of God's love, I was being transformed right before my family and friends. Not all of them liked the changes I was making in my life. I remember wanting to be baptized and being ridiculed about it. Since I had been christened as a baby, some members of my family wanted to know why I thought I needed to be baptized again. I was rather young in my faith, so I didn't know how to answer all their questions. More and more, I felt awkward around my family. I had to fight the shame I was feeling for being different. But I knew I wanted more and more of Jesus.

When I played sports, I asked God to strengthen me and help me play to the best of my ability. At school I began to offer up my classes to the Lord, and He started to bless my grades.

I remember teaching the whole basketball team every praise and worship song I knew as we rode on a bus to away games. Soon those songs became our favorites.

I shared Jesus with one of my closest friends in choir, and she accepted Jesus right there in a public high school. So many lives were touched because Jesus had changed mine, and I wanted to tell the world.

God uses us right where we are, no matter how young we are in Jesus. So I say to the youth of this world, "Don't let anyone think little of you because you are young. Be their ideal; let them follow the way you teach and live; be a pattern for them in your love, your faith and your clean thoughts" (1 Tim. 4:12, TLB).

We were created to have a wonderful, intimate friendship with God and then to give that love away to this hurting, dying world. That is why Jesus came. He came for the sick and the brokenhearted. He came to bring healing and restoration to each of our lives.

If I could encourage you to do anything, it would be to get on your knees and give Jesus everything—all your hurts, all your failures, all your successes and all your disappointments. Let Him have total control of everything and everyone in your life.

As I began to throw out parts of my old nature and exchange them for a new nature, even my countenance began to change. I was reflecting the image of God in my life. My old life was full of lust and shame and wrong thoughts and desires. (See Ephesians 4:22–23.) To reflect the image of God, I had to be continually renewed in my attitudes and thoughts. Then I could put on the new nature of Christ and clothe myself with right living and a holy life.

To exchange the old for the new, I could see the advantage of being in a best-friend relationship with the living God. I wanted to spend more time with the Lord, getting to know Him by reading the Bible daily and letting His love wash over my life.

I did make time every night to read my Bible. I was surprised to discover how much the Bible spoke directly about a situation with which I was struggling. Through reading the Word, I found out how to honor my parents, even when it was hard. I learned how to turn the other cheek and respond correctly. I found out that life would never be fair, but it was how I responded to the injustice that affected my future.

Sometimes this was so hard that I thought I would never make it. To complicate matters, I never knew from one day to the next how my dad might respond to something I did or did not do. There were days when I would do my household chores and things would go smoothly, but I never received praise or encouragement. Then there were days when I forgot to do something, and I would feel shame overwhelm me. During those times, I felt that no matter what I did or how hard I tried, I would never be good enough.

To deal with this shame, I would slip silently off to my room with my head hanging low and play the piano for hours to escape the pain I was feeling. Throughout these times, God would meet me in my broken state and touch my life. Somehow, just pouring my heart out to God through worship brought peace back into my life, and I knew I would make it. Worship became a constant expression in my life. No matter what I did, my heart wanted to bring honor and glory to God. As I prayed and cried out to God, He heard my cries and healed me right where I needed it most.

After I made Jesus the Lord of my life, I had the ability to love the Lord with all my heart, soul and mind. As I understood how deeply God loved me, I could give that love away.

When I am at the market, God may prompt me to encourage the checker. At the gas station, God may direct my eyes to a little girl sitting nearby and tell me to go share His love with her.

We were all created to love God first and to let Him have first place in our lives—above our families, spouses, children, jobs, even our churches.

Whatever you do, let Jesus be Lord of everything in your life. If you put your relationship with the Lord first, you will be able to love others genuinely, and they will accept it. You will be able to love your husband whether he is meeting your needs or not. You will be able to love your children even when they blow it. And you will be able to love your family members even if they are not in a place where they can love you in return.

As I began my new life in Christ, I started to attend a local church with some friends. It was as if the blinders were removed from my eyes, and I began to see differently. I became suspicious that my dad was living a hidden lifestyle of sin.

One day in particular, I felt that way. I came home from school unexpectedly and caught my dad sitting close to a man on a love seat, and they were holding hands. He quickly jumped up and acted as if nothing had happened. I ran to my room in a panic.

Oh, my God! This can't be happening! I felt such hideous shame come over me that I wanted to die. *Where in the world could I go? Where could I hide? Who would ever believe me?* I hurried to get my things. I rushed away, telling my dad I had to go somewhere. He nervously let me go, but his eyes were filled with pain.

Racing into town in my car, I was so angry I couldn't even cry. I yelled at God, "How could this be happening to me? Why do I have to deal with this on top of everything else I'm dealing with?" I loved my dad so much, and I wanted him to understand how much Jesus loved him. But his deep sin and shame was blocking the path. Before long, I was certain my dad was living a homosexual lifestyle.

I was taken off guard. *How could I live at home with my dad living a secret life or live with my mom whose new husband I loathed?* From that time on, I determined to keep this secret to myself. The only other person who knew was my boyfriend, who had a family member that lived the same lifestyle.

At this point in my life, I was in deep turmoil. I desperately wanted to escape the pain, so I tried to get drunk. I took one sip of beer, and it made me so sick I thought I would throw up. I would never drink again. At this point I was not receiving any physical love or affection from my mom or dad and, having acquired an unhealthy view of sexuality from them, I began to look for love in all the wrong places.

At that time, I became distracted in my Christian walk. I was sixteen and had a boyfriend who told me that as long as we didn't have intercourse, everything else was okay. He lied, but I was so starved for attention and so naive about everything that I believed him.

I wanted to be loved genuinely, but he took advantage of me. Many times in this relationship, I would come home feeling violated and dirty. My own choices filled me with shame, yet I didn't understand what was right or wrong. I began to withdraw and, in a way, disconnect from reality. Soon I gave up trying. Both of my parents had made bad choices in their sexuality, and I was ashamed and confused. I had no one to turn to, so I existed for a time stuck somewhere in shame.

Two years was enough time for me to understand that something was deeply wrong in my life, and I needed a change. I knew the guilt and shame I was feeling from this relationship was not from God. I felt tormented, and the only relief came when I spent time with Jesus. During these times, I could feel God wooing me back to my first love relationship with Him. I felt safe and secure whenever I read the Bible, worshiped or prayed. Deep within me, I knew I needed to break it off with my boyfriend, but I felt trapped.

Graduating from high school became my ticket out of town. Now I could escape and leave my past behind. God even opened up a door for me to attend a Christian college. I eagerly jumped at the chance to live a new life, away from my family and boyfriend.

I saw this opportunity as a fresh start for my life and thanked God for rescuing me. No one would have to know where I came from or what I did or what my family life was like. I could hide my shame from everyone. No one would know but me.

Freedom was just around the corner—or so I thought. As I began college, I enjoyed everything about it—the atmosphere, my friends, my education and all the opportunities I needed to grow in my walk with Jesus. I knew I didn't want to get married until I was at least thirty and out of college with a strong career behind me. I broke up with my old boyfriend and vowed not to have another one for quite a while. Although the shame I felt from that relationship clung to me, I believed if I didn't think about it, I could move on.

In my first year of college, I met a nice guy. He was so genuine in his faith, and he loved to worship the Lord. I was attracted to his heart, and I wanted to know what made him so secure and happy. I secretly watched him from afar. I admired his strengths, which shined in his deep-set eyes. He always had a warm smile to greet everyone, and his zest for life was contagious. He seemed to have this knack for making people feel at ease no matter who they were. He had a passion and security in his relationship with Jesus that I had never seen in anyone. He was friendly and kind, and I couldn't help but feel drawn to him.

I spent a lot of time hanging out with him, just being friends and having fun. Eventually people asked me if I liked him. "No," I reassured them, "we're just friends. But whoever marries Mark Smucker will be incredibly blessed."

Then one day I was walking up my dorm stairs, and it was like I'd been hit over the head by a frying pan. I *did* really like Mark, but I didn't think I was good enough for him, especially with my family background and my own shameful past. But God challenged my thinking and asked me, "Why not be the one to marry Mark Smucker?" At that moment, I decided he was the one for me. Now, how could I be sure he knew I was the one for him?

As I began to spend more time with Mark and his family, I realized I had never seen a husband and wife treat each other the way Mark's parents did. His mom, LeeAnn, loved and served her husband, Willard, and he responded to that love. They were very affectionate, and I could tell it was genuine. Watching their marriage up close began to heal my mixed-up view of what family was all about. I couldn't believe what was happening to me. My decision to never marry was dissolving. *Could I really trust someone enough to be married to him forever?* But God was healing my view of marriage. I had to exchange my old ideas for new thoughts of what marriage is really all about.

I had never felt like I wanted to get married. In fact, I never really thought about what it would be like to fall in love and be married. I found myself watching Willard and LeeAnn really love each other. What I saw began to restore my faith that a marriage can last a lifetime and two people can be genuinely happy with each other.

Over the course of the next two years, Mark and I got engaged. During that time, I had more time to watch a Christian family in real-life situations.

They were grass seed farmers, so when summertime came, they were in the heat of harvest. I thought for sure that if someone's temper were going to fly, it would be during this season. What I observed, however, was a family that worked together. It was LeeAnn's job to keep everyone well-fed and happy, and it was Willard's job to keep the farm running smoothly. Everyone did his or her job with little or no stress. There was no screaming, and yet everyone was under pressure to do his job and do it well. Their family's financial success depended entirely on these three summer months. If everyone did their part to the best of their ability, then God would surely do His part. It was amazing to watch Willard run their farm and watch Mark and his two younger brothers respond to him with such honor. I had never seen young men respect their dad like this.

At first, Willard was quite intimidating to me. He was quiet and never said much unless he had something to say. I was almost afraid he didn't like me. But before long, he began to tease me, and I began to relax and start to enjoy my first example of a godly dad.

It felt funny enjoying someone else as a dad. I felt like I was betraying my own dad in a way. I knew I didn't want Willard to replace my dad, but he had a peace about him that my dad didn't have. I watched him carefully. He was mysterious to me, yet I was drawn to the security I felt when I was around him. He seemed so wise and calm. I asked myself, *Could a family really be this good?* I was beginning to see hope for my future. I really wanted a family like this one. No, they weren't perfect, but they sure enjoyed each other. I knew deep in my heart that this was what I had prayed for since I was a little girl—a family that loved and cared for one another instead of yelling. *Was God answering the cries of my little-girl heart?* I had to answer, *Yes, He was, in the biggest way possible.*

On our wedding day, moments before my dad was to walk me down the aisle, I found out my pastor had led him in prayer to receive Jesus as Lord of his life. When this news filtered into my dressing room, I could hardly contain myself. Had I not been in my wedding gown, I would have jumped for joy. I was in awe of God for giving me such an incredible wedding present. I was beaming. There was no time to cry tears of joy, so my bridesmaids and I joined hands, rejoiced and began to thank God together in prayer for my dad's salvation.

Here, on the most important day of my life, Dad would share this moment with me in such a special way. I couldn't contain my happiness when my dad took my arm to walk me down the aisle. As we gazed at each other, I saw a twinkle in my dad's eyes that I hadn't seen before. He was being transformed right before me. He grabbed my hand and squeezed it so hard. Soon we were walking down the aisle to the wonderful hymn, "Holy, Holy, Holy." We both felt washed clean by the redemptive power of Jesus. God had taken our family, with a life of shame, and in one divine encounter, removed that shame and began restoring it with His glory. What an answer to prayer! Over the years, I had begged God to see both my parents come to know Jesus before I got married. My mom rededicated her life to Christ while I was in college, and now my dad was born again. God fulfilled one of the deepest desires of my heart that day. I was marrying the man I loved and watching God begin to transform my family.

That day, I realized God was putting a new name on me spiritually, as well as literally. Although I had suffered injustice as a child, God was redeeming that back and pouring out a double portion of His blessing upon my life through the man of God I was marrying.

After that, I understood more about God's deep love and compassion for us all. He wants each one of us to experience a double portion of His grace upon our lives. For this to happen, we must have the faith to believe that God loves us and cares about each of us individually. He knows where we are broken and hurting. We cannot hide our pain from God. He has been right there with us through every defeat, disappointment and discouragement.

God's love for me brought healing to my heart and ushered in my salvation and my parents' salvation. But we all have to choose to accept God's grace and forgiveness, which will open the door to our faith. Then we can believe that God will wipe away our past, full of sin and shame, once and for all. As we become new creatures in Christ, the old things will pass away and our fresh new lives will begin. (See 2 Corinthians 5:17.) We will become brand new people with a hope and a future because God has a plan and a purpose for all of us. (See Jeremiah 29:11.)

To make these exchanges with God, we must begin simply by humbling ourselves in prayer. Please stop and pray with me now, and start making your own shame exchanges.

Dear Jesus, I give You my heart. I give You all my crushed hopes and shattered dreams. Please, take my shame and exchange it for Your grace and mercy.

Please forgive me for my sins and draw me back into that first love relationship with You. Jesus, here is my past, full of sin and shame. Please take it from me today and give me a new life full of freedom and joy. Thank You, Lord. Amen.

Little did I know how important these small prayer exchanges were going to be in my life. If I had known the depth of shame still lying dormant in my heart at that time in my life, I wouldn't have wanted to face my future. But God, in His enduring love for me, never gave me more than I could handle.

THREE

The Power of
His Grace
Produces Faith

Life seemed to get easier for a while. We were living in wedded bliss our first year of marriage, focusing most of our attention on each other. We saw our families, but only for short periods of time. We were seeking peace and seclusion by enjoying married life and not worrying about our families. We were self-centered, but we were young and in love.

My dad's lifestyle hadn't changed, but he tried to attend church and read the Bible. I wasn't mature enough in my Christian walk then to help my dad out of his bondage of sin. But I prayed for him, and because we lived three hours away, I'd call him or send him encouraging notes. Nothing seemed to help. He was trapped and tormented by shame. Eventually, I went into denial because I didn't know how to help him.

At this time, I was on a personal journey of my own to freedom. However, I didn't really understand how much healing needed to take place in the depths of my heart. I had covered up so much for so long by simply convincing myself that it never really happened. Unfortunately, I still had anger deep down inside, and sometimes it would raise its offensive head.

Every now and then, I would blow up over the smallest things. It didn't happen often, but when it did, I felt out of control and ashamed of the way I had acted. Mark would love me through it and try to understand what was happening, but I could never pinpoint why I would get so mad and lose it. I believe I learned a behavior pattern after watching the way my parents responded to situations. That pattern didn't go away, even though I made right choices in my life, such as marrying the right person. My standard response to pressure was to stuff it until it would explode inside of me. The tension would mount so high that I couldn't control it, and then the force would need to be released. I would unleash my anger on someone, and then I would feel bad, but I'd also feel better. When the tension was released, I could say I was sorry and try to press past the deep embarrassment and shame I felt because I had blown it.

I was at a crucial place in my life, and I needed a turning point. I knew I didn't want to respond in anger, but I didn't know how to stop it or how to deal with it when it did come. Later in my life, I learned that anger is the emotion of shame, but then I just felt trapped. So I began to pray for God to start healing me.

As months went by, both Mark and I felt a strong urge to be ready and available to do something new. Neither of us recognized what that would be, but we began to pray about it together. Soon after, a team came to our church from Youth With a Mission (YWAM) and shared a vision of young people going all over the world to tell others about Jesus. We also learned that YWAM held Discipleship Training Schools (DTS) around the world to train young men and women to serve on the mission field.

During the teaching phase of DTS, students would get sound biblical teaching on the nature and character of God. One of YWAM's primary goals is for students to genuinely know God and then make Him known to others. Mark and I were immediately impressed that DTS could be the answer to our prayers. We couldn't wait to learn more about God. We were both hungry for more of Jesus, and I was desperate to change my life.

The YWAM team left a pamphlet with us, and we noticed that this particular training school would be in New Zealand. We began to pray about it. The more we prayed, the more we felt called to go. We shared our new vision with Mark's parents and asked for their blessing. They were supportive and excited to see us launch into missions.

But two weeks later, tragedy struck. Mark's dad died of massive heart failure. He was only forty-three years old. Everyone was crying. I tried hard to be strong, but I felt abandoned once again. *How could God take away my new dad? I was just getting to know him. We were finally beginning to relax around each other.* I decided I wouldn't love again. It hurt too much. I was too shocked to grieve. It was a confusing time.

We were twenty-two and ready to go off on a new adventure, but how could we leave in the midst of such sorrow and great loss? *Why would God send us to the other side of the world when our family was falling apart? Did we make a mistake when we heard we were to leave?*

After a few days of trying not to love again, I could see the results of living that kind of life. I would never have a good family if I stopped loving Mark. I didn't want that for us or for our future children. I didn't want my marriage to end like my parents' marriage did. I wanted to live in a loving family. I had so much life to live. God surely would help us through this deep loss. No one could ever replace Mark's dad—not for any of us.

The foundations of our family members' lives were tremendously shaken, but we had to try to return to the normalcy of life and move on. Death has a way of making life stand still as you find ways to cope with the pain of your loss. Mark's mom grieved so deeply, we were concerned for her. For a time, our lives revolved around trying to help Mom. Mark and his brothers put their own grief on hold because their mom was so fragile. She had lost her most treasured friend in the world, and she didn't know how she could move on.

At that moment, our hearts were bleeding. We all needed love and support. We didn't know how to help one another. We got along day by day the best we knew how. In the back of my mind I wondered, *Would we ever fulfill our destiny and go into all the world?* We put that dream on hold and dedicated ourselves to helping with the farm and keeping the family together.

Running a grass seed farm at age twenty-two is no easy task, especially since Mark's dad had kept everything in his head. Mark had to rely on everything he had learned about farming from his dad and the faithful team of employees he had. God certainly helped bless our business that first summer without Dad. We made it through and even made money. Then a painful decision was upon us.

Our family's emotions still ran high. We were all suffering so much after Dad's death. Mark and I weren't equipped to counsel his mom or even begin to help her through her intense loneliness. On top of all that, we were still dealing with my dad and his bondage to sin. Mark and I felt we had more than we could handle. We felt overburdened, and we struggled just to keep peace in our own lives.

Given all this, Mark and I decided the best thing for us and his family was to follow the guidance we received from God and go to New Zealand for Discipleship Training School. We had to step out in faith and take a risk, not only for us, but for both of our families. Someone somewhere had to equip us and help us find the answers that would bring comfort to our shattered lives.

That fall, we headed to YWAM New Zealand. We still felt a struggle raging within us and yet a deep sense of peace about going. *Why was God asking us to go to the other side of the world?* New Zealand is on the other side of the Pacific Ocean. That was as far as you could get from home, or at least it felt like it to us and our families. Not only did we have to have faith to believe we had heard God correctly, but then it was time to put our faith into action and let God have His way with us. We would have to trust Him to help our families in their greatest hour of need.

That was one of the toughest and most unpopular decisions we've ever made. We had to trust our faith and believe for what we could not see yet. As Hebrews 11:1 says, "Faith is the confident assurance that something we want is going to happen. It is the certainty that what we hope for is waiting for us, even though we cannot see it up ahead" (TLB). But we knew deep in our hearts that God was worthy of our trust and faith. Jesus is who He says He is, and He will do what He says He will do. We must believe the truth— the Word of God—and that truth will set us free.

All God was asking of us was to pray, and He was promising to do the rest. He tells us in His Word that "You will find me when you seek me, if you look for me in earnest" (Jer. 29:11–13, TLB). God was stirring us to look to Him and no one else to meet our needs. God never promised us that we would not have pain and hardship in our lives. He promised that He will walk with us through the deepest, most difficult times.

God holds our future in His hands. Let Him provide the agenda for your life, and let Him lead you as you fulfill His mission for your life. When you do this, God will give you a future and a hope, even when you cannot see what is ahead or on the horizon. Peace comes. Joy comes. Understanding comes. When you are willing to put your faith and trust in God, He will meet all your needs abundantly.

When we got to New Zealand, we began to see the marvelous plan God had for us. Deep healing started to take place in our lives. We had set aside this time to learn more about God and ourselves. We were freed from responsibilities at home, and we were left to concentrate on our relationship with God and with each other. For the first time in my life, I felt I could concentrate on just being Laurie Smucker. No one was telling me what to do or how to do it. They were just letting me soak in all the foundational teachings about Jesus. I was saturating myself with everything there was to learn and writing it down as fast as I could.

Several weeks into the lecture phase, an instructor named Matt Rawlins flew in from Singapore. He taught that what we value will determine what we are going to do. Do we know who we are and what we were made for and where we are going? He taught that if we look at our schedule for the week and see where we spent most of our time, we will find that which is most valuable to us. Mark and I were incredibly challenged by what Matt shared.

We learned that Matt was originally from Salem, Oregon, close to our hometown. It felt like God had brought a little bit of home to us just to bless us.

Immediately, Mark and Matt hit it off. We also found out that he, too, was going through a broken period in his life. His mom was dying of cancer, so Mark and Matt spent much time sharing their grief with each other.

He told us that if we ever needed help in our business that his dad, Duane, could help us. As he left, we thanked him for everything and thought we would never see him again. We didn't know then that God was forming a divine plan for us to be a family two years later.

During this time with YWAM, incredible restoration took place in our lives. We developed a deeper walk with Jesus as we became equipped to preach the gospel and to help both of our wounded families.

After outreach to the Philippines, we flew home, and within a few hours of our arrival, we encouraged Mark's mom to do a Crossroads Discipleship Training School in

Kona, Hawaii, for adults who are at a crossroads in their lives for one reason or another. We told her she should do something for herself because she was at such a crossroad since her husband's death. She immediately said this was exactly what she needed. LeeAnn left for YWAM that fall.

What happened over the next two years was a complete intervention of God in all of our lives. LeeAnn left the Crossroads DTS and came home a changed woman. God had ministered to her, and some amazing healing took place in her life. No longer was she dealing with the pain of her past. She left her past behind and pressed on to be all that God had called her to be.

Sometimes pain and shame have similar attributes. Whether we suffer from the loss of a loved one or we suffer pain through shameful experiences, the enemy will try to hold us captive in the grip of our past. LeeAnn was now as free as we were to move into the future that God had planned for her. By that time, two years had passed since Willard's death, and she wanted to serve God in YWAM. She began at the closest YWAM base, in Salem, Oregon. There she met a man named Duane Rawlins and fell head over heels in love. She came home after serving there one week and said, "I have met the man I want to marry."

Needless to say, we were concerned about who this man was. Then she told us his name, and we almost fell over. *Could this be the father of Matt Rawlins, whom we met in our Discipleship Training School?*

Yes, Duane was Matt's dad. His wife, Betty, had passed from this life to eternity. Duane and LeeAnn had prayed individually for mates who would understand their pain of losing a loving spouse. Then when birthdays and anniversaries from their former mates came around, they could comfort each other. Does God not move sovereignly and mightily, even in the midst of our pain and suffering? As a family, we gave them our blessings to be married several months later.

Now they fly all over the world to share their story. God knew exactly what they needed and what our two families needed. He had a plan for all of us, and yet we had to have faith in Almighty God and trust Him that He would restore our families back to health. It gave me renewed hope for my family. I could only pray that God would restore my family and give us all a second chance to really love one another.

Mark and I are so grateful that we obeyed God during one of the hardest times of our lives. God met us where we needed Him most. Now we have two wonderful families that are knitted together.

It's never easy to blend two families together, even when everyone loves Jesus and no matter how great the two families are. Adjustments need to be made, and that takes time. Every one of us has opinions and personalities to bring into the mix. But the key lies in loving God and letting God show us how to love one another.

It has taken some time, but we all enjoy one another's company. Some of us are closer than others, but we've learned to just relax and let relationships develop as they come and not try to force anything on anyone.

When you love God with all your heart, it is easy to look past everyone's inconsistencies and all the emotions we humans have been designed with. All of us have different feelings, passions and gifts. That is why God made each of us so complex and unique. He loves that about us. He has given each of us special gifts, and every one of them is important and complements the others.

Romans 12:6–12 speaks of the different gifts God has given each of us individually. Some of us will prophesy. Some will serve, and others will teach. Many of us will be asked to give of our finances. Others will be put in charge of people around them. Several of us will comfort others or simply just love one another. Whatever your gift, I encourage you to be all that God has called you to be.

Stand strong in your beliefs and be passionate about your love relationship with Jesus. Walk where God wants you to walk. Cry out to God to show you what your individual gifts are.

It is much like putting the last piece of a puzzle in. When the puzzle is complete, it forms an awesome picture. If you or I never put our puzzle piece into the picture, the picture will not be complete. It will always be unfinished. Don't you hate it when you finish a puzzle and you find out there is one piece missing? You begin searching high and low for it. If you find it, there is great joy and relief because now you can finish the puzzle.

That picture is a beautiful reflection of how God wants the church to be. If we love God and put our faith in Him, He will show us what our gifts are and how to walk them out. When we withhold our gifts from God, it hurts Him, it hurts us and it also hurts others.

For the church to be a reflection of His glory displayed for all the world to see, everyone must put their piece into the puzzle.

Let God have His way with you. Let Him show you how He loves you. Put your trust in Him, and He will give you amazing grace in any situation, much like He did when He put our two families together.

Only God's grace could produce so much faith in our lives during these difficult times. However, no amount of faith could have prepared us for what was to come.

FOUR

Father to the Fatherless

By this time, Mark and I were preparing to start a family. Just two weeks before my delivery date, we learned that my dad was terribly sick. In my heart, I knew he had AIDS. It seemed that whenever we went to see him, he was sick with something. His immune system wasn't working properly, and somehow I just knew what was wrong. I think God prepared me so I wouldn't be so shocked.

My suspicions were confirmed. My dad was dying of full-blown AIDS. It was a blow that took my breath away. I didn't know if I could stand by and watch my dad die such a painful and debilitating death.

I felt frozen with fear. *How could I help when our first*

child was coming into this world? Whom could I tell, and whom could I trust? Where could I run, and where could I hide? I couldn't think or even rationalize.

I was overwhelmed with grief. Yet at the same time, the joy of our firstborn was upon us. *But how could we rejoice?* I wanted to run away from it all, but I knew I needed to spend time with my dad to prepare him for eternity.

When we went to see my dad in the hospital, I felt a responsibility to walk him through repentance and forgiveness. I wanted to make sure he had made everything right with God. I remember taking the long walk up to his hospital room and wondering how he would respond to me. I was so afraid to face my dad and the unknown.

When we got to his hospital room, there was a big sign on the door saying we must robe up before entering this room. They used so many precautions. This placed fear in my heart just standing by the door. So I stood there, nine months pregnant, putting on gloves, a mask and a robe. *Was this disease so contagious that I couldn't even hold my dad's hand without gloves on?* This was in 1987, so AIDS was just hitting the United States. And AIDS was hitting my life head on. *How could I go in to see my dad dressed up with all this stuff on?* I felt so sterile and cold that I wanted to scream and cry out at the same time. *How could my dad feel the love of Jesus through my gloves or see the love of Jesus through my mask?* All that was left uncovered were my eyes.

We mustered enough strength to open the door and go into his room. I saw my dad lying there. His eyes met mine. Never before have I felt so helpless. I wanted to burst into tears. I wanted him to know how much I loved him and how much I cared about him. Yet he spoke first.

He was humble and broken. With tears in his eyes, he squeezed my hand and told me how sorry he was for all the pain he had caused me. With all my heart, I wanted to throw myself into my daddy's arms and cry like his little girl. I felt so constrained because of the fear of AIDS that I held back from hugging him. I felt sterile robed up in the hospital gown and gloves. I'm sure my dad felt even more isolated. I'm sure he felt much like a leper did in Jesus' day.

I will never forget what happened in those next few moments. God's power moved in that hospital room. Something happened in the Spirit, and both of us cried and felt tremendous peace.

I knew that unless God healed my dad, he would die a painful death, and I would lose him physically. And yet, he had come to a point in his life where he knew what mattered most—to see complete healing in my heart and in the hearts of his other children. My daddy knew what being a father was all about at that moment. He looked beyond his own pain and grief, his sorrow and shame, and held his little girl's hand and repented. When our eyes met, we understood how we felt about each other. Something miraculous took place in a daddy's heart for his daughter. That day, for the first time, I heard my dad say he was so sorry about everything. He was asking for my forgiveness.

Repentance and forgiveness usher in the presence of God like nothing else I know. We felt the power of God's exchange from a daddy's broken heart to a daughter's shattered heart. As we prayed together for God's forgiveness, I felt that peace that passes all understanding. Here I was, absolutely huge and ready to bring a new life into this world while I was watching a disease take my dad's life. *How could I ever have enough strength to have this baby?*

As I gave birth to my firstborn child, it was a bittersweet moment. We shed tears of great joy amid tears of deep sorrow. *Would my dad ever be able to hold my son in his arms?*

I was overcome with emotion, but I knew God was by my side while my heart was breaking.

> The Lord is close to those whose hearts are breaking;
> He rescues those who are humbly sorry for their sins.
> The good man does not escape all troubles—he has
> them, too. But the Lord helps him in each and every
> one.
>
> —PSALM 34:18–19, TLB

God will be by your side, too, when you walk through those broken areas of your life. He will be your complete source as you walk through the pain.

Sometimes we wish we could flee from the pain and the endless torment going on deep within our souls. Getting through each day is enough to cause us to feel like we are gasping for breath. We feel smothered in grief, and our only relief comes when we can sleep and keep our minds from thinking.

But God is there, and His amazing grace will be overwhelmingly sufficient to get us through the long hours of the day. He rescues those who are sorry for their sins. As my dad repented, I felt freedom exchange between a daddy and a daughter. Repentance and forgiveness frees people, and then they can and will love again.

My dad and I both faced never growing old together. I faced the fact that my children will never know either of their grandfathers, that I will never hear my dad say, "She looks and acts just like you did when you where little."

I looked back at the pain of my past and realized that my past was not my future, that God had so much more for me, and it was yet to come. God wanted me to use the pain of my past and let Him heal me and teach me more about His character. He wanted me to see that the loss of a loved one produces in us the compassion to feel and know more about the unfailing love of Jesus. I was just beginning to heal.

As the months went by, my dad's health deteriorated. He had come home and was under hospice and family care. I knew my job was to take care of my dad's spiritual condition, not his physical condition. I knew my dad would never want to put one of his children or grandchildren at risk medically. We drove to my hometown every other weekend. It took me about two weeks to recover every time I went to be with Dad and my family. Each of his six children had his or her own way of dealing with Dad's disease. Two were the caregivers, two were supportive but really couldn't take care of Dad, and two just couldn't deal with this particular disease taking his life.

During this time, there was much tension and conflict in our family. Again, I felt so desperate. I would come home from seeing my dad and spend the next few days just trying to get out of bed. I was racked with grief and agony from watching my dad deteriorate right before my eyes. I was the youngest and the only one living out of town. I felt torn between living in two worlds. *Was I doing the right thing? Was I disappointing my family? How could they understand how I felt when they were just trying to get by themselves?*

My emotions were on a roller coaster. I was up and down, weeping and laughing. I felt guilty for enjoying my son's first year while my family was hurting deeply. Never really knowing what to do to help, I felt frozen with fear. Death can tear a family apart, or it can draw it closer together. I was praying for God to hold us together long enough to make it through this major storm that felt like a tornado.

During the months that followed, Mark and I felt called to join Matt and Celia Rawlins in Singapore to help with the YWAM base there. We prayed and even asked for my dad's blessing to go. He assured us we should go, yet I felt torn. *How could I leave my dad and my family at such a crucial time as this? How long would my dad hold on to life?* As the months slipped by, we waited to see how my dad would do. He began to deteriorate so fast that most of the time, he didn't even know we were there. It was as if we had lost him as he slipped into a coma-like state. We didn't know how long he would live this way. It could be months or even longer.

After postponing our trip for a month, we prayed, "Lord, if we're just gone two days and my dad dies, we know we were obedient to do Your will." I remember surrendering my will to the Lord that night and crying out for His guidance. A few days later, after our son's first birthday, we flew to Singapore. It took thirty-six hours to get there. Aaron had only slept five hours during the entire trip, so needless to say, we were exhausted and emotionally spent when Matt picked us up at the airport.

I thought to myself, *What in the world am I doing? Why did I fly clear to Singapore, and what will I do here?* I felt empty of myself as I said, "Not my will but Yours be done, Lord."

Two days after our arrival in Singapore, my dad slipped into eternity. It was all over. *Was it our obedience to God that released my dad to finally die? Or was it just our complete sur-*

50

render to do His will for our lives? We may never know.

As we flew home, I pondered that prayer we prayed just a few days earlier. Here we were traveling thirty-six hours to get back home with a one-year-old baby. *How would we ever make it? Oh, God, please give us the strength we need to get home and walk through this funeral.* We put a new name on short-term missionaries.

Before the funeral, there was time for family from out of town to gather. As the food was brought in and uncles and aunts arrived, we prepared to say good-bye to Dad.

The night before the service, I became physically ill. I was vomiting and having violent stomach cramps. I would sip only water, but everything would come up. I prayed, "Lord, I flew all this way, and now I'm not going to be able to attend my own dad's funeral?"

My husband rushed me to the hospital, and they gave me some medicine to stop the vomiting. Before we arrived back at my mom's house, she was getting sick. The next day we learned that fifteen other family members had gotten sick. It was a miracle that I made it to Dad's service. I was weak physically and emotionally. *How would I ever stand in this weak state and make it through this service?* The cry of my heart was simply to stand.

Amazingly, God has a way of rescuing us even when we think we cannot take much more. I understand that scripture, "And the peace of God, which surpasses all comprehension, will guard your hearts and your minds in Christ Jesus" (Phil. 4:7, NAS). I felt so much peace and strength that I knew it had to come from the Lord. Once again, He met me right when I needed Him most. Even in my most desperate hour, He was right by my side. I was so grateful.

Without even knowing it, I had exchanged my weakness for His strength, just as His Word says in 1 Corinthians 4:10. I was able to stand and be strong through the whole day.

Funerals are never easy, but this one came with much relief. I knew my dad was in heaven. His physical body didn't hurt anymore. He had a new body and a new name, and he was standing before God in peace. He would never suffer pain again. He would never suffer shame again. He had made his final exchange with the Lord. My Dad traded this life on earth for eternal life spent worshiping the King of kings.

We still miss him terribly. On Father's Day, Mark and I always feel lonely for our dads. But we laugh as we imagine them in heaven, celebrating life together, enjoying the very presence of the most high God. Who really won? I think they did.

Although my dad was at peace, the year that followed his death was a battle for me. In one sense, I felt abandoned and racked with sorrow. *Who would be my dad, and how could I ever tell anyone how my dad had died?* I felt deep shame sweep over my life as I covered up and tried to hide the shame of his death. I sank into deep depression not really understanding how to get through it. I rarely talked to anyone about it—not even Mark. A part of me just hoped it would go away.

After the death of my dad, the pain I felt wasn't physical; it was emotional. The two feelings are worlds apart. Physical pain generally will go away in a few days. Deep emotional pain can cripple you, and it can be a struggle just to get up and walk.

Some mornings, the grief was so intense that I went

through the motions of the day not really having any purpose. I was in survival mode.

At this point, after losing both of our dads, I looked to the closest men that I admired most to fill that void in my life. My pastors were wonderful men of God and said they would be there for me. One of them came to my dad's funeral.

However, I was so paralyzed with pain that I was dying inside, and I couldn't even reach out and let them know how I felt. I needed someone to reach out to me. I just couldn't communicate that to either one of my pastors.

What happened next in my church shook me to the core. Our church split because we had two pastors going in opposite directions. One had an evangelistic heart for the nations and the city around him. The other pastor had a heart to pastor the flock at home and strengthen the community.

Because of their differences, the eldership at that time had to decide who would be head pastor. Both pastors were to stay on board, but one would be serving the other's primary call for the church. The pastor with the evangelistic heart was chosen to be the main pastor. The other pastor decided to leave to start a church with the vision to pastor the sheep.

It got messy. I felt like I was on a bloody war field, and I came away shell-shocked. I was frozen with fear. Time stood still. Questions ran through my mind. *Where would we go, and what would we do? Do we stay at our home church, or do we leave and listen to all the negative talk going around town?*

One hundred of our closest friends—the kind that felt like family to us—had left the church. We were wounded people with broken hearts, and God was doing a work to purify us.

Mark and I were committed to staying where God had called us, so we hung in there for the long haul. But I felt abandoned and fatherless. *How could God let both of our dads die, and then have our church split in such a short span of time?* I felt like I would never be able to trust anyone again. I felt let down, disappointed, confused and tormented. *Who would be the father to the fatherless children?*

I remember going to church and just going through the motions. I didn't think people noticed. They probably thought that somehow I would find the strength to make it myself because I was young. I failed miserably. I couldn't escape the pain of shame, and it seemed to be crushing me.

What happened over the course of the next year made me feel as if my heart were being ripped out. I knew God was asking me to give it all to Him, but I felt so vulnerable and afraid. *How could I give God that which was so precious to me? How could He fill the void of being a daddy?*

I spent weeks searching and crying out for the answer. When healing begins, it seems small and insignificant at first. I remember lifting my hands after many weeks went by in my attempt to surrender. I began to soften and cry and let the pain that was squeezing my heart release some of the pressure.

Then one Sunday, my pastor shared that if we wanted more of Jesus in our lives, we would have to give Him more of ourselves. We would have to give Him everything—all the good with the bad, all the pain, disappointments, failures, successes, everything. My pastor said we needed to surrender even those painful areas of our hearts so Jesus could release His healing power in our lives. For a moment, I thought, *Could it be this simple?* All I had to do was surrender everything to God, and He would come and rescue me. I decided it was worth the risk, and right there I surrendered everything to Jesus.

I remember putting my hands together, lifting my heart up to the Lord, and giving all my grief and pain to Jesus. I let God know that, if He wanted to be my daddy and if He was the only daddy I would ever have again, He would be enough.

I knew God would never die, leave me, fail me or let me down. I knew He would greet me every morning and be with me at all times. I knew He would always love me.

I had made another shame exchange. I traded my sorrow and pain for His love and grace. Complete peace happened at that moment, and it felt like a ton of bricks was lifted from my shoulders. No more being strong. No more striving to make it on my own. I had raised the white flag and surrendered.

As I sat down, a man in our church headed toward me. He had been listening to God speak to him on a hunting trip, and the Lord asked him to be a father to the fatherless. The fatherless one was me. He had waited months to come to me, and now seemed like the right time. He had no idea what I had just done. But God did.

As Veldon shared his heart with me, my eyes began to well up with tears. I listened intently as he shared how God had spoken to him in the middle of the night in Mongolia and asked him to step in and be a dad to a fatherless young woman named Laurie.

I was stunned and speechless. I didn't know how to respond. I sat there with my mouth hanging open for a few seconds. As I responded, I told Veldon what I had just done. In an awkward way, we embraced for the first time. It felt good to know I was so special to God that He brought me an adopted dad so quickly. Veldon happened to be my husband's dad's first cousin. He would be like Mark's dad in stature and personality.

God had moved within minutes of my surrendering of my heart. I was overcome with joy. I had exchanged all my shame about my dad, and here God was already giving me a new earthly dad. I was shocked and very emotional.

Since that day, I have seen my new earthly dad almost every week. It has been years, but I still look forward to his hugs every Sunday. God restores everything this world tries to take from you, and His exchange rate is always a double portion. Jesus loves to heal the brokenhearted and bind up their wounds. I'm so glad I surrendered that day. True healing began to melt my hardened heart. Restoration of my life began because I relinquished all my hurt.

I was beginning to live.

God is longing for us to give it all to Him so He can give back to us.

You see, sometimes God is longing for us to give it all to Him so He can give back to us. It was there all along. He was just waiting for me to be ready to receive what He had planned to bless me with.

Sometimes God cannot move until we do. Sometimes we hold the keys to unlock the closed doors of our hearts. God is waiting and ready to move. He wants to see where our hearts are. Will we give Him our heart, soul and mind? Will we give Him our all in all? Will we hold nothing back from our heavenly Father?

I urge you to give Him your heart. Give Him all of you. Don't hold anything back from God. Let this song be your heart's cry:

> *Lord, I give You my heart.*
> *Lord I give You my hopes and dreams.*
> *Lord, I give You my heart.*
> *I give You everything.*
> *I give You all of me.*
> *I give You everything.*
>
> —LAURIE SMUCKER (2000)

Surrendering all to the Lord will happen again and again in our lives. Something will come up, and we will have to allow God to have complete control over our lives and circumstances. Sometimes we will take back something we had already exchanged with God and try to carry it all over again. Constant exchanges with God have to be made for us to grow in our intimate walk with the Lord.

There is a scripture that goes along with what happened in my life. God tested Abraham's faith and obedience.

> "Take with you your only son—yes, Isaac whom you love so much—and go to the land of Moriah and sacrifice him there as a burnt offering upon one of the mountains which I'll point out to you."
>
> When they reached the place God had told him about, Abraham built an altar there and arranged the wood on it. He bound his son Isaac and laid him on the altar, on top of the wood. Then he reached out his hand and took the knife to slay his son. But the angel

of the Lord called out to him from heaven, "Abraham! Abraham!"

"Here I am," he replied.

"Do not lay a hand on the boy," he said. "Do not do anything to him. Now I know that you fear God, because you have not withheld from me your son, your only son."

—GENESIS 22:9–12, TLB

I know I would have an incredibly hard time sacrificing any of my children. But Abraham had his eyes on God, and he was more concerned with obeying his Lord than keeping anything from Him. How about you? If God tested your faith and obedience, would you be willing to lay it down and keep your focus on Jesus and not on the situation? Are you willing to lay down that which is most precious and valuable to you? What are you withholding from the Lord?

God didn't want Isaac's physical death; He wanted Abraham to "sacrifice" Isaac in his heart. Do we love God more than our families? Are we willing to "sacrifice" them in our hearts and turn them over to Jesus?

It took me a year to make the decision to turn my broken heart over to Jesus. If I had known what was waiting for me, I would have done it much sooner. But God is a patient God, gladly testing us to strengthen our character and make us more like Him.

If you obey God, He will provide. When I finally surrendered my hurt and pain over being fatherless, God provided another father.

Abraham withheld nothing from God, not even his only son, and God provided a ram caught by its horns in a bush. So Abraham sacrificed this ram instead of his son.

Jesus is the ram that was sacrificed for us once and for all. God did not spare His only Son; instead, He was sacrificed for us so we can be spared from eternal death and receive eternal life.

When God asks you to give Him everything, do it. Run toward God, lay everything down, and don't pick it up again. Jesus gave His all for each of us. Shouldn't we in turn give Him everything?

Matthew 10:37–39 says we should. "Anyone who loves his father or mother more than me is not worthy of me; anyone who loves his son or daughter more than me is not worthy of me; and anyone who does not take his cross and follow me is not worthy of me. Whoever finds his life will lose it, and whoever loses his life for my sake will find it" (TLB).

If we hold on to the things of this world, we may relinquish all that Christ has waiting for us today and tomorrow. The world's rewards come up short-handed and empty. But God has many rewards waiting for those who place Him above all else in their lives.

God will even be faithful in rewarding all your unseen deeds. He sees all the little things you do that no one else notices. So think about what unselfish gift of love you can give to someone without expecting something in return. The Bible says, "I will bless you with incredible blessings and multiply your descendants into countless thousands and millions, like the stars above you in the sky, and like the sands along the seashore. They will conquer their enemies, and your offspring will be a blessing to all the nations of the earth—all because you have obeyed me." (See Genesis 22:17–18.)

What a promise! Our children and grandchildren also

will honor and obey God. They will face and conquer their enemies. When we obey, as Abraham did, we will receive incredible blessings. When we obey God, people's lives will be impacted because of our faith and obedience. I wonder what blessing is waiting for you as you turn everything over to your Savior.

FIVE

His Eye Is on the Sparrow

As the years go by, tears come to my eyes.
As I watch our lives, oh, how time seems to fly.
As the seasons change, one thing will remain,
My only source of strength,
My only secret of peace is to worship the King
*   of kings.*
Pour over me, oh Lord, with Your unfailing love.
Pour over me, oh Lord, with Your cleansing blood.
Pour over this valley. Holy Spirit, pour over our
*   families.*
Come and fill our cup. Overwhelm our lives, as You
*   pour over me.*

—LAURIE SMUCKER (2000)

This song is a personal expression of how God has poured over my life in the last twenty years. So much has changed and transpired through making shame exchanges a constant part of my life.

I am blessed with a wonderful husband and three beautiful children. We make our home on a grass seed farm in the Willamette Valley. My husband and I are a major part of the leadership in our church through worship, eldership and Bible teaching.

I have seen how God takes shame from a person's life and exchanges it for His double portions.

Throughout the years, I have made many shame exchanges with the Lord without a single regret. Each time I make an exchange, I become more like the image of my Lord and Savior. Every time I surrender my shame, He releases me into a new level of His glory.

We are all changing from one degree of glory to another. The amount of freedom and blessings we can experience in our lives depends on our ability to make these shame exchanges. The degree with which we experience freedom is also key to walking in the call that God has placed on our lives.

Over the years, deep healing and restoration have brought me clearer insight into the heart of God. He longs for all of us to know how He really feels about us.

When I personally discovered how much Jesus loves me and how often His thoughts turn toward me, I had to change my way of thinking.

Many times I would be reading my Bible, and God would just drop an incredible word in my lap. One time that comes to mind was when I was sitting on my bed reading Ephesians 2:8 and I found out I was saved by His grace; I didn't have to do anything to earn it. That salvation was a free gift, and all I had to do was receive it. I was overwhelmed with the knowledge that Jesus gave me a gift because He loved me.

Other times, God would touch my heart during worship, and I would feel His presence washing over my life. Sometimes, I would lift my hands in surrender because Jesus was all I had.

He *was* all I had. Jesus was the only One who knew my deepest, darkest secrets. When I was in high school, I felt so ashamed about my dad's lifestyle that I couldn't tell anyone, not even my family. I was afraid to tell my youth pastor for fear of getting kicked out of the church. I didn't want to tell my friends because I was afraid they would tell someone and then the whole school would know.

Many times when I was struggling so intensely, God would intervene on my behalf. I remember crying out for His help at times because of my difficult situation.

I used to go to my room, play the piano and worship to escape. I would picture myself being laid at the feet of Jesus. I was broken, weary and overwhelmed with the weight of carrying this big, dark family secret. Jesus would bend down and pick me up and just hold me in His warm, loving arms. The pressure I was carrying would be removed, and I could relax and embrace His love.

Worship seemed to make life's circumstances look so much smaller. When I worshiped God, He would always lift me up and fill me again so I could go on.

Since that time, I have learned why God met me so quickly when I didn't even know what I was doing. When we pour ourselves out at the feet of Jesus and we are empty, lonely and desperate, He rushes to our side to pick us up and fill our cup.

I felt like the woman who anointed the feet of Jesus and wiped His feet with her tears. Here she was, a woman of the world, deeply ashamed but willing to rush in, uninvited, and pour oil over the feet of Jesus.

She wasn't worried about what people would say about her. She wanted only to be close to Jesus. I love the response Jesus gave her: "Therefore I tell you, her sins, many [as there are], are forgiven her—because she has loved much. But he who is forgiven little loves little" (Luke 7:47, AMP). Jesus also said to the woman, "Your faith has saved you; go (enter) into peace [in freedom from all the distresses that are experienced as the result of sin]" (Luke 7:50, AMP).

Just like this woman, peace would fill my empty soul, and I would rise up and be able to face my difficult family life.

There was a time when I was far more worried about what people would say about *me*. When you have walked in deep shame as I have, you have a terrible self-image. You imagine you are not perfect in what you do or in how you look.

Therefore, one of the shame exchanges I had to make was to quit speaking so much shame over myself. I never felt comfortable with how I looked or confident in what I did. I really didn't know how to curl my hair or wear make-up, so I would hide the feminine side of me with the tomboy look. I didn't like to draw attention to myself, so I chose not to dress up. Furthermore, I didn't know how to receive compliments. I felt awkward and embarrassed during my adolescent years.

I'm sure many of you can relate to these feelings of

self-hatred. Somehow, we never feel that we will fit in or that we are even good enough to try.

Catch yourself the next time you have wrong thoughts about yourself. Ask yourself, *Where are these voices coming from? Are they from God or from Satan?* If you can, stop at this moment and ask God where the deep wound is that keeps you from believing what God really thinks about you.

No matter how much talent you may have or how beautiful you may be, you will never feel good about yourself until you understand what God thinks about you. If we rely on man's opinions to be our source of who we are, we will get a false view of ourselves.

I remember asking God to show me how He viewed me. His view changed my impression of myself. He gave me a picture in my mind of myself as a little girl running and jumping through a field full of daisies and buttercups, my blonde hair blowing in the warm spring breeze. When I stopped to pick the flowers to make a daisy chain, someone caught my attention. It was Jesus. He waited with great anticipation, His arms outstretched, as I ran to Him.

I felt so warm and secure in the arms of Jesus. He held me close to His chest and began to speak to me softly.

He said, "My daughter, you are the apple of My eye. You bring Me great joy as I watch you live and grow. I love everything about you. I created you. I formed you. I have great plans for you. If you live in Me, I will live in you. If you abide deeply in Me, I will abide deeply in you. Dwell in My presence, and I will dwell in you."

For the first time in my life, I felt a deep sense of hope that I could become all that God wanted me to be. I didn't want to leave that moment, but Jesus promised me we would have many encounters along the way in my life.

I encourage you to stop right now and spend time with Jesus. Ask Him how He feels about you. If you are hurting so much that you cannot even dream for yourself, go to my field of daisies and buttercups. Picture yourself as a child running into the arms of Jesus. Just rest there awhile until He tells you how He feels about you. You will be pleasantly surprised.

We can speak so much shame over ourselves by talking bad about how we were formed. Well, God doesn't create junk. He does not create two people anywhere close to being the same shape or size. We need to stop speaking shame over ourselves and start asking God how He sees us, what He thinks about us and why He created each one of us so uniquely.

The enemy tries so hard to deceive us into seeing only negative images of ourselves. Then we feel we will never measure up to the world's standards. Who said we had to? God never did.

So many of us are in a personal struggle with ourselves about what we look like or what the world says we should look like. All we can see are our imperfections. We don't like this or that about ourselves. If we only looked like the pictures in the magazines or on television, then we would be happy. Or, if we just lost ten more pounds, then we would feel better about ourselves.

Some of us go to the extent that we want to alter our bodies. We would like someone else's nose, or less in the hip area and more somewhere else.

When I was growing up, I developed a cyst on my nose. You couldn't notice it unless I turned sideways, and it looked like a small bump on my nose. It didn't help matters that my last name was Rose, and it rhymed with *nose*. I was teased and named "Laurie Rose with a bump on her nose."

It hurt to answer all the questions about why I had a bump on my nose. It hurt to hear that I would be cute if only I didn't have that bump on my nose.

I remember when I finally had it removed. I came back from surgery with two black eyes and a nose packed with gauze. There was a small piece of clear tape covering the outside incision. I had to wait two weeks before removing the tape and gauze. My friends were trying to picture what I would look like after I removed the tape.

The countdown was on, and I remember thinking, *What will it really be like not to have a bump on my nose? Will I really want to be noticed?* I was nervous, yet so excited.

After two weeks had passed, I went to the bathroom that morning to get ready for school. I remember peeling the tape off my nose and turning my head sideways to see what I would look like without that bump I had grown so accustomed to.

I felt pretty for the first time in my life. It seemed that overnight, I had grown from an ugly duckling to a beautiful swan. I couldn't wait to get to school to see what my friends would say. I didn't mind all the attention, and I felt confident in how I looked for the first time.

At school, people didn't know what to say. I think they were all in shock. It's like when someone gets braces off and you see the person for the first time with straight teeth. My friends were so used to seeing me with that bump on my nose that it became a part of who I was and how they saw me.

Now even I saw myself differently, and I began to try

and uncover the shadow of shame I felt because of that bump.

I had read in Psalm 139 that God knows every little thing about me. He knew when I was formed and that I would develop this cyst on my nose. He knew how it would make me feel, and yet how it would enhance my character if I allowed it to.

He knows all about you, too. He knows your likes and dislikes. He knows what will bless you and bring you great joy. He knows about all your little quirks and what makes you tick. He knows all this because He created you.

He wants all of us to be thankful for His creation. We were in God's mind before our parents knew anything about us. God watched us develop in our mothers' wombs, and He watched in utter amazement.

At the moment of our birth, all heaven rejoiced at the miracle of another child of God. I'm sure God enjoys dreaming up our future and planning ahead for us. He has so much He wants all of us to enjoy. He is waiting to show us all His dreams and plans.

Put this book down right now and just stop and dream a little. Try to comprehend that you have a God who loves you so much that He has a plan and a future for you. We need to look ahead and believe with all our hearts that God does have a future and a hope for us. But first we must seek Him with all our hearts. (See Jeremiah 29:11.)

As the years have gone by, I struggle less and less with how I look or feel about myself. Now there are only about a dozen days a year that I struggle with my self-image. Usually this happens on Sunday mornings when I'm getting ready for church. Those old feelings come up and nag at me when I know I have to be in front of a lot of people.

I have trouble deciding what to wear, and after about five outfits, I finally stop and say, "Okay, God, show me what You see." Then, when I have finally given up all hope of looking good, God will bring encouragement to my mind. Then, and only then, can I leave my home filled with a grateful heart for being the person God created me to be.

Some of you are thinking, *It can't be that easy.* Yes, it can be, and it is. God's ways are easy to understand if we will only open our minds to His Word and His ways.

Isaiah 55:8–9 shares, "For My thoughts are not your thoughts, neither are your ways My ways, says the Lord. For as the heavens are higher than the earth, so are My ways higher than your ways and My thoughts than your thoughts" (AMP).

God's knowledge and wisdom is far greater than any man's or woman's. Let's ask God to give us His thoughts about ourselves. God imparts special gifts in each of us, and He wants us to use them for His glory.

Some of us are so worried about what other people think that we are too afraid to step out of our comfort zones. *Why are we more concerned about what men think than what God thinks?*

I know people who have to ask advice from a dozen people before they will make a decision. They really don't want their advice, they just want someone to agree with them or pat them on the back.

When I go to my pastor for counsel, he always listens to me, then shares his heart. I listen to his wisdom carefully because I trust him. In the end, he always encourages me to seek God and let Him show me what I should do.

I think that is good advice. If we had more people in our lives telling us to run to Jesus, we would make wiser decisions sooner.

I have been in many situations where I have asked for advice. Although people will give me advice, it is up to me to pray and make the final decision. After all, I will have to pay the price for any choices I make. Sometimes, even when we make good choices, it can come with a cost. But I have learned that God will ultimately bless any choice He asks me to make.

One example is when God asked me to honor my parents after I got saved. That meant I couldn't fight with them, even if I was right. It was hard, but worth it. The tense atmosphere would always clear between my dad and I when I responded in honor. His response would soften, and many times he would try to make it up to me by taking me out to eat or to a movie. If I dishonored him by yelling back, we would get into a huge fight. Then nobody would win. I quickly learned that I would reap benefits by responding in honor.

If we are always consumed with what people think of us, whether it's a family member or a church leader, it puts our eyes on man and off God. Man will make mistakes and give us wrong advice or say wrong things. But if we listen to God's voice and not our own or others, He will guide and direct our lives and all our decisions.

Satan will always try to invade our minds and cloud our decisions. He will try to place a seed in our minds called "fear of failure," which makes us afraid to try because we're afraid we will fail. God is always there when we fall down or fail. He is always there to pick us up and put bandages on us. We will never succeed in anything in life if we don't try.

Matthew 10:29–31 says, "Are not two little sparrows

sold for a penny? And yet not one of them will fall to the ground without your Father's leave (consent) *and* notice. But even the very hairs of your head are all numbered. Fear not, then; you are of more value than many sparrows" (AMP).

Dwell on that scripture for a while. When you think about how God really feels about you, it will give you the strength to try and even to fail. If we don't step out and take risks in our lives, we will stay protected in our comfort zones because it's safe and predictable.

As a family, we have had to learn a big life lesson on how we do things. I'm one of those people who like things orderly and not messy. It can drive me crazy when people leave things lying around, especially in my home. The fact that I always want things done a certain way can drive my family nuts. We all had to learn that chores can get done, but in many different ways and time frames. For example, when I ask my children to do simple chores, such as dusting or vacuuming, the job will get done, but maybe not up to my standards.

I have had to allow my children to do things in their own way and relax my standards a little. On the other hand, they have had to improve on their housecleaning skills and learn the proper ways of doing certain things. As they get older, I can raise the bar a little and expect more from them because they have learned from experience.

As a parent, it is easy to heap shame upon our children. Sometimes we expect them to do simple tasks as well as we would. When we expect perfection from our children, we can drive them from us in the process.

I have learned that if I want my children to grow up and be secure in who God created them to be, I must encourage them many more times than I correct them. If all I did was tear them down, even when they really tried, fear of failure would overtake them and at least one of them would give up trying altogether. Another child might strive so hard to please me that he would be consumed with being perfect and trying to earn my love and acceptance.

If you think back over your life, you will see how much more God has encouraged you than disciplined you. When God disciplines us, it is out of His great love for us. He doesn't demand that we do things His way. God has set up guidelines for us to follow, and the choices are ours.

This is exactly how we should parent. We should set up guidelines for our children to follow, but we must also remember to encourage and build them up along the way.

When children learn to walk, you hold their hands before you let them try to walk on their own. As parents take their hands away, the babies will fall down many times before they begin to walk. As children learn how to balance, they no longer need their parents' help.

It is the same in our relationship with God. We can either take our Savior's hand and let Him guide us when we are stepping out of our comfort zones, or we can stay right where we are and never risk failure or embarrassment. Clearly, we all need to know that sometimes we are going to fail, and God is going to be right there to pick us up.

One example of this in my life is playing the piano in public. I have played the piano for years, and yet I have always held back playing in public because of the fear of making a mistake and embarrassing myself in front of people. One day, God whispered in my ear that He was the One who gave me that gift and asked me why I wasn't using it to bring glory to Him.

He was nudging me out of my comfort zone. I grew uncomfortable as God challenged me to step out and play in church. God wanted me to fly, but I wanted to hide.

It is much like a mother eagle teaching her young to fly. She begins to stir up the nest and actually tears it apart. The baby eaglets must think their mom has gone crazy. She also begins to flap her wings to send air into the babies' wings so they can begin to feel how to fly.

Next she will knock one of them out of the nest, soar underneath it and catch it on her back. The mother eagle does this over and over again until every one of the eaglets can fly.

Like the mother eagle, God has much higher plans for us. He wants us to fly! God will do what it takes to knock us out of the nest so we will trust His ways and learn to fly.

As I began to play in public, I heard a lot of negative sounds in my head. I always thought I sounded terrible and that I made too many mistakes. I would get so nervous that I could barely play. I was ready to quit when people began to encourage me and tell me I was sounding so much better.

I thought, *If I sound better now, then how bad was I?* God gently corrected me. He said. "Listen, and let me show you what I hear."

> Behold, you are to them as a very lovely [love] song of one who has a pleasant voice and can play well on an instrument.
> —EZEKIEL 33:32 (AMP)

Since this time, I have played in public for many Bible studies and retreats. I have recently had the privilege of

73

playing and worshiping on a video for a ministry called *Restoration*, which is based out of our church. This ministry is a twelve-week study that keys on people who are broken and wounded and in need of deep healing in their lives.

On this video, I have shared some personal songs that were born out of my most intimate worship times with my Savior. Many lives have been touched by them. I am blessed to be a part of this ministry.

It's important to see, God will promote and encourage us better than anyone else can. I wasn't expecting to lead worship on this video. I was blessed that they even asked me. God isn't concerned with how great I sound or how talented I am. He is more concerned with where my heart is and how it can touch people's lives.

If we are to use our lives to bring glory to Him, then we can bring joy to the heart of God. God looks at the world's sins twenty-four hours a day, seven days a week, and His heart breaks over our brokenness. If we can bring joy to His broken heart by stepping out and using our gifts, then we need to be bold and step out in faith.

Many times, I will try something new in my private worship times. God is a creative God, and He loves to meet me wherever I am or in whatever I am doing.

I love to worship God, and I love to jog. So I have combined the two. When I jog, I pray and listen to my favorite worship tapes. There is nothing like having a fun time with God and being touched by His glory. Often I will be running along, and I will open up my hands at my sides and lift them slightly upward in worship. Instantly, I will feel God touching me and releasing His glory over my life for the next thirty seconds. When I drop my arms and get back into the rhythm of running, I don't feel the same presence of His Holy Spirit.

We can experience His touch on our lives throughout our days. No matter what we are doing, we can always stop and physically express ourselves to God in some way.

When I'm cleaning the house, I always have great upbeat worship music playing. When I'm driving my car, I'm either listening to worship or Bible teaching tapes.

Everyday life can have its ups and downs. We all will experience success and failure in our lives. We all will experience victory and defeat. No matter what season we are in, God wants to win our battles for us. All we need to do is lift our hands in complete surrender to Him.

Remember the story in Exodus 17:11 where Moses held up his hands? As long as Moses did this, the Israelites were winning, but whenever he lowered his hands, the Amalekites were winning. This story is a picture of complete surrender and worship. Moses knew that, to win the battle, his eyes needed to be totally on God. When he became weary, the Israelites began to lose as he lowered his arms to his sides. Moses also had friends at his side to stand with him and help him keep his arms raised.

Oftentimes our everyday battles are won through our complete surrender and worship. But many times, we lose our focus because we try to do things our own way or by ourselves.

If we focus on Him and His glory, everything else falls into place. We won't fear failure. We won't want to be anyone else but who God created us to be. If we focus on God's purpose for our lives, the circumstances we are in won't look so overwhelming.

The next time you feel afraid, focus on God's love instead of fear. The Bible says, "Perfect love casts out fear" (1 John 4:18, NAS). If you let fear be your focus, then it will overwhelm your mind, and the devil will try to steal that place in your heart.

This has helped me to overcome fear. I always try to envision myself in the warm arms of my heavenly Father. When I am in His strong arms and I feel His overwhelming love for me, all fear is then washed away.

God is always waiting for us to run to Him. All we have to do is call out to Him, and He will instantly be near. He longs for us to seek Him so He can be found. The cries of our heart tug at the heart of our heavenly Father. He longs to rush to our side and comfort us.

My relationship with the heavenly Father is much like my relationship with my children. When my children cry out in pain, I am instantly there to love them and pick them up. I don't waste a second wondering if they need my help. I instinctively run to their side.

Another way to stay focused on God's purpose and plan for our lives is to focus on His glory instead of our shame. If we focus on the shame of our past, then we will never leave our past behind.

When Jesus died, He took all our sins and nailed them to the cross once and for all. He bore all our shame and dishonor. It is beyond my comprehension to try to understand all Jesus did to set me free. But I have personally experienced God's glory replacing the shame in my life. Let your thoughts focus on His glory, and allow Him to replace your shame.

Often I am surprised at how the devil will try to persuade me that my shame is too big, and I shouldn't let anyone know about it. This is a lie that can keep me covered up with its shadow.

It's like when you're lying in the sun, enjoying the heat penetrating your body, and a huge cloud forms and blocks the sun. Soon you get cold and you either have to put warmer clothes on or go inside where it's warm.

Shame works the same way. When we expose it to the light, our heavenly Father can take it from us and replace it with His glory. If we choose to cover up the shame and hide it from the Father, we will continue to walk in the shadow of shame.

When you give more of your shame to the Lord, He can release a greater measure of glory in your life.

This is stated in Ephesians 1:18: "I pray also that the eyes of your heart may be enlightened [opened] so that you will know what is the hope of His calling [the future He has called you to share], that are the riches of the glory of His inheritance in the saints" (NAS).

We were created to reflect God's glory to the world.

God wants to open the eyes of your heart so He can give you a future and a hope and let His glory reflect from your life. We were created to reflect God's glory to the world.

Isaiah 43:7 says, "Even everyone who is called by My name, whom I have created for My glory, whom I have formed, whom I have made" (AMP). We are called to give an example of the power of God's love to the hurting people of this world. God takes our broken lives and allows His light to shine through our cracks so we can touch others. We are constantly put on display for the world to see the power of God's grace in our daily lives.

When we reflect God's glory, we cannot help but be noticed.

I have firsthand experience with this. One time when I was at the gas station, I saw a little girl crying outside by her friends. I felt a nudge in my heart to go see if this little girl was okay. I obeyed God's urging and cautiously walked over and shared with the girl who I was and what church I attended. I asked her if she needed help, and she began to pour out her heart to me.

She was staying with her aunt, and she missed her dad very much. I encouraged her to ask her aunt if she could call her dad to talk. Then I asked her about her mother. She told me she missed her, too, but she hadn't seen her in more than a year.

My heart broke for this innocent ten-year-old. She reminded me of myself. She was hurting and broken and wounded because of her parents' failed marriage—something she couldn't do anything about. I then asked her if she knew Jesus and if I could pray with her and her friends. She said yes. As we began to pray right there on the sidewalk, I knew I was being Jesus to this little girl. I felt His touch on my life as I took this little girl's hands and prayed for her.

We all need to live our lives to reflect God's image to others. We may be the only Jesus they will ever see. How do we get more of His glory in our lives? To have more of God's glory, all we need to do is ask. Come before the Lord and ask Him to saturate your life with His glory. Give the Lord no rest, and ask Him to release more of His grace into your life so you can give that grace away to others. Immerse yourself with the love of God. Spend time reading your Bible, and ask God to remove the effects of shame from your life.

You'll see that God is the only One who can do this. Think back on that time when you felt that no one cared and that your world was crashing in on you. No matter what anyone said or did, it didn't help fill that void in your life. Even then, God never gave up on you. He was wooing you back to Himself. He was broken over your situation in life, for it wasn't what He intended for you.

I remember the intense pain of my parents' divorce and how that left me with feelings of abandonment. I felt so alone and helpless, just as many of you are feeling right now. I felt angry, which caused me to rebel and seek something to numb the pain.

The world has nothing to offer us in our hurtful places. Only the Father can mend our broken hearts and restore us back to Himself.

The power of His love can bring more healing into your life and into the lives of others than you could imagine. Never give up hope. Never give up faith. Never give up on love. Never give up on others. Never give up on yourself because God will never give up on you. Because the greatest gift that was given to us from our heavenly Father was the unselfish gift of His only Son, who died for all our sin and shame.

Please don't wait another minute to exchange your shame for His glory. Don't allow your painful past to hold you captive any longer. Break free, and begin to fly and experience the exhilaration of living your life with purpose for the King of kings. He will lift you up and overwhelm you with His great love. He is so proud of you, and His heart leaps with joy over who you are becoming.

He will fill you and then pour you out on this broken, dying world.

As you continue to make the transition from shame to glory, think about how you would answer these questions. Take the time to press through your thoughts and allow God to begin the healing process.

Something to Think About

- What does He think about His creation (you)?

- Explain what Isaiah 55:8–9 shares about God's thoughts versus the world's thoughts.

- What is the seed Satan has tried to plant in our minds?

- What is God concerned with? Our gifts, talents or what?

- Where does our focus need to be?

- What does Ephesians 1:18 speak to your heart?

- Whose image are we to reflect?

- What three areas should you never give up on?

SIX

Unshakable Kingdom

Now you know what will happen if you exchange your shame for His glory. But one year, as our family was doing a huge remodeling on our house, God gave me a fresh revelation about what happens to us if we do not deal with the sin and the shame of our past.

When Mark and I began the renovation, we had to tear out all the old stuff, such as bathtubs, sinks, tiles and flooring, before we could replace it with the new stuff. Even the roof had to be removed before we could replace it with a second story and a new roof.

I remember tearing the shingles off the old roof and thinking, *I have never worked so hard in my life.* My back was killing me, and I just couldn't wait until this job was over. We were sweaty, dirty and tired, yet satisfied that we had accomplished the job. I had a new respect for my roofer friend that day as it shed some insight on how hard a roofer really has to work.

As we cut the original rafters off our roof, our house looked like it had been hit by a tornado. We lay in bed that night praying it wouldn't rain and wondering if we had made a huge mistake.

Questions were running through our minds. *How could our one-story, ranch-style home, which now looked ruined, turn into a beautiful, two-story farmhouse?* We both agreed that we either had made the worst mistake or the best decision of our lives. We also knew the damage was done to our original house and there was no turning back.

Cutting off shame from your life is like cutting off your roof. In both cases, you are exposed and uncovered. Sometimes it feels as if you have been hit by a tornado, but you know deep in your heart that you never want to go back to living the way you had been. It feels like the roof has been raised in your life, so you can be free to step out and move on and build upon a new foundation.

After I got saved, I knew immediately that I was never to return to the party lifestyle. The standard of how I lived my life had been raised. I was making a 180-degree turn-around. I would never again go down that lonely road of trying to numb the pain of my shame by getting drunk. I was pressing forward and beginning the building process.

As the months continued during our house remodeling, we tore out old doors and moldings and knocked out walls to make more room.

Just as we had only begun to demolish our old house,

some of us have only just begun to rip out the shame in our lives. Before you can replace shame, you must tear it out and make room for God to come and bring healing into your life.

Over the next several months, the walls went up on the second floor, then the rafters and finally, a new roof. We were all covered again and free from worry about the rain destroying anything.

After you exchange your sin and shame and begin to rebuild your life, you must base the foundations of your life on the truths in God's Word. I know no other greater tool than the Bible to replace shame because it contains the truth that will set every captive free.

As our house began to take on a new look and personality, your countenance will begin to change. As people drove by our house, they began to anticipate the transformation. No one in the neighborhood could have been more excited than we were as we saw our dreams coming true.

In your life, people will start to recognize the changes you are making. They may even ask you, "What is so different about you?" or "What happened to you?" No one will feel better about the changes in your life than you will. At this point, you begin to realize that you are affecting people because of the transformation of your life.

During the house project, I was in awe that God gave me such amazing builders. You also will be in awe of God as you build your life on Jesus, the master builder.

First Corinthians 3:10–13 tells how a skillful architect and master builder laid the foundation and how another man built upon it. We took great care in selecting our architect and builder. We knew that without expert builders, our house could end up looking worse than it did before we began the project.

This works the same way in our spiritual lives. If we have any other foundation except Jesus, we will have to tear down the old and rebuild on the One and only true foundation.

We also knew we needed quality building materials so we would pass each inspection. If we were to use cheaper products or cut corners, the building wouldn't meet code, and we would be forced to tear down and start over. This could be costly and time-consuming; it would not be wise or efficient. Just the same, when you are rebuilding your life, you want to do a quality job the first time around.

Tearing out sin and shame is a process that takes hard work and effort

Tearing out sin and shame is a process that takes hard work and effort. When you first get saved, you exchange your sin and shame for salvation. You feel light as a feather because the burden of carrying your sin and shame has been lifted. You walk around feeling better than you have in your entire life. Nothing seems to faze you because you are no longer carrying your sin. Maybe for the first time in your life, you realize what price Jesus paid on the cross to set you free and give you salvation.

At times, however, we may return to the comfort of our past. That is where we are wounded, and we are emotionally stuck there. This is where we must exchange our shame. If there are deep wounds in our lives, we must turn them

84

over to God so He can heal our brokenness. This can be painful and difficult to do. We have to bring the wound to the surface and deal with the pain before we can exchange it. Then we must surrender our hurt and shame to the Lord and allow His healing touch to wash over our lives.

Many times there will be a need for repentance and forgiveness. This is the only pattern I know of that will set you free. If you are not willing to surrender your pain and repent or forgive, you will have to go around the mountain again and have to deal with the same shame over and over again.

No one wants to tear down what they just built and have to redo it. I want all of us to exchange our shame and never go back to the past. Unfortunately, it doesn't always work that way.

I have found that if I can give my shame entirely over to the Lord the first time and not go back and pick it up again, I will be set free. But when I withhold my shame from the Lord, I stay stuck until I surrender it completely.

We also need to realize that these shame exchanges can come with a cost. Seldom are they easy. But I have found any price I have to pay to get free is worth it. An example is the time I needed to forgive my parents for the pain they caused me through the divorce. There was a price for that freedom. I could no longer respond to them out of dishonor because the Bible says to honor your mother and father. Many times I would have to leave the room and hug a pillow and scream because they made me so angry. But soon I was set free from responding to them out of my anger and hurt. And in return, all I felt for them was deep love and compassion. I had made an exchange, and God replaced my anger with His unfailing love and mercy. Then my life began to be built upon the truth of God's Word. This solid foundation will stand under any test that comes.

Once we completed rebuilding the house, we could start the finishing work. New plaster was put on ceilings and walls, but it was messy and hard to clean up. Fresh coats of paint began to bring light into each room, but the paint fumes almost consumed us.

Just like remodeling, cleaning up shame can feel messy and even smell bad at times. Anytime you return to your old ways of doing things, your life will get messy very quickly. Your emotions will try to override any common sense, and you will walk in shame again.

I have returned to the shame of anger many times. When something comes my way that has a negative impact on my life, I often respond in anger. This response can have a messy effect on the lives of the people I am around at that time. After this encounter, before I can move on or before the people I have hurt can move on, I must repent and ask for forgiveness to be set free and to set them free.

No one can really make us angry. It is an emotion we can control. We allow anger to consume us, and then we explode, which can adversely affect the people whose lives we touch. It is a flesh and spirit exchange. We may have to stop whatever we're doing and pray, "Lord, please take my anger and remove it, and please replace it with Your mercy and love."

Quickly try this pattern of exchange the next time you want to respond negatively. It cannot hurt the situation; it can only help it. Trade your unforgiveness for His forgiveness. Let Jesus replace the dishonor you're feeling with His honor. The next time you feel disgraced, let God replace it with His grace.

Before long, Mark and I were ready for new toilets and sinks to be put in our house, along with new flooring and carpet. Likewise, as we go on in our lives and begin to walk out of shame, we are ready to add the finishing touches to our lives. Our lives are ready to be filled with the Holy Spirit so the power can be turned on. We are being transformed from the old man to the new man.

By this time, my house was starting to take on a new appearance with certain characteristics. I could hardly believe my eyes as the lights turned on for the first time and shined on our new home. I was utterly exhausted, yet completely blessed and thrilled beyond my imagination. I felt God had blessed me far beyond anything I could ever have dared to ask for or even dream of. This new farm house of mine was way beyond my highest prayers, desires, hopes and dreams. (See Ephesians 3:20.)

You may feel you hardly recognize yourself because you have changed so much. The past is so far removed that you can barely remember the effects it had on your life. You are beginning to live.

Soon after the finishing touches, we began to fill our house with new furniture to make it comfortable. We went to the store so we could fill the refrigerator with food. Soon we had everything we needed to begin living in our new house.

It is the same with shame exchanges. You must fill the empty space with something of God, or you will be open and vulnerable to the attacks of the enemy.

As we began to decorate our home, it took on a new look and style. New life was coming to this old house, and it was finished and looked all swept, clean and ready to move into.

We did all this work to remodel this home and make it like new again. But what would happen if we never moved back in? What would become of our lives if we removed the shame but didn't fill it up with the things of God?

Jesus paid the ultimate price of laying down His life for our sin and shame, and yet we don't want to receive it in some areas of our lives. We withhold different pieces from God because it hurts too much to turn it over.

If the house remained unoccupied, vandals could come and destroy it, or thieves could break in and steal all that was inside, leaving it worse off than its original state. This is what the enemy will do in your life if you do not exchange your shame.

Just as the newly remodeled house had no life in it, the same is true for our lives when we ask the Lord to remove our sin and shame and then don't allow Him to fill it with something new.

I think this scripture best relates to what will happen to us if we do not deal with our sin and shame.

> But when the unclean spirit has gone out of a man, it roams through dry [arid] places in search of rest, but it does not find any. Then it says, I will go back to my house from which I came out. And when it arrives, it finds the place unoccupied, swept, put in order, *and* decorated. Then it goes and brings with it seven other spirits more wicked than itself, and they go in and make their home there. And the last condition of that man becomes worse than the first. So also shall it be with this wicked generation.
>
> —MATTHEW 12:43–45 (AMP)

Jesus was describing the attitude of the nation of Israel and the religious leaders at that time. They were cleaning up their lives on the outside so they would look good, but they were not filling their lives up with God or changing their hearts on the inside.

If we rid ourselves of the sin in which we are involved but never fill that emptiness back up with the cleansing love of God, we are leaving too much room for Satan to enter back into our lives and hold us captives of our past. The enemy could come in and affect us seven times worse than before.

What is your attitude about your sin and past shame that you are carrying? Are you cleaning house in your life and not filling it up with God? We must hate our sin and despise it to the point that we want to get rid of it forever and never look back to the shame of our past again.

When you fill a house with a family, it becomes a home. Love and laughter spill over into that home, and the place takes on life because of people. Memories are built, happiness and heartaches shared.

As a family grows, so do the memories. Your home takes on character and sentimental value. You may never want to sell it because it holds so much of your life inside. As your children grow up and leave home, grandchildren will come along soon and bring fresh, new joy to an empty nest.

This is true with our lives. Is your life full of shame and disorder, or is it somewhere in the process from shame to glory? Are you frustrated because there is too much junk from your past swept under the rug that you just don't want to deal with? Or is it all swept clean and put in order?

Even if your life is cleaned up, if it is not filled with God, Satan will try to move in. Satan is always trying to get us to return to our past. If we stay stuck there, we won't be as effective in our lives or in the lives we touch.

One day as I was cleaning my house and putting it back in order one more time, God nudged at my heart. I had cleaned the kitchen and the bathroom, and I was ready to vacuum and finish up the job. God whispered, "What do you have?" I said, "A clean house."

You see Jesus had been waiting for me all morning to spend time with Him, and I kept putting Him off until I got my house in order. When I finished cleaning house, then I had time to sit with Jesus. During the first five minutes of my quiet time, He didn't shame me, but He showed me how He felt about me. I wrote a song about His love for me and put chords to it in only fifteen minutes.

Jesus didn't really care how clean my house was. He cares about my love relationship with Him. Of course, He wants me to take care of all that He has given me, but He wants to be first in my life.

Some of us like everything in order before we can sit back, relax and enjoy life. But that will never happen. Housecleaning or something else will always be there.

Jesus will always be there, too, but His return on our investment is better than a clean house. He has something to give us and something to speak over us. All we need to do is take the time to be with Him and quiet ourselves long enough to hear His voice. If we begin our day with Jesus, the day will always go better, no matter what difficulties we may face.

We can continue to clean house or busy ourselves with work or pour ourselves into ministry and make everything look good on the outside. We can even fool lots of people doing it because we have learned how to cope in our difficult situations. Or we can slow down long enough to deal with our pain and let God heal us.

Nothing is hidden from God.

God knows what is going on inside your heart. He knows every broken area in your life. He knows about all your disappointments and failures. Nothing is hidden from God. He knows your deepest, darkest secrets, and He also knows your deepest longings. He knows what was done to you in secret, and it broke His heart.

Jesus died for our sin and shame. He paid the highest price. He doesn't want us living in shame for the rest of our lives because He knows the pain it causes us. We must be serious about repentance so those oppressive spirits won't move back in. We must continue to trade our shame for something new that God has for us. We never want to take back our past sin or shame. We must get rid of it and never look back again. We need to fill our lives with God's overwhelming love and mercy. We must serve God with an obedient heart and fill up on His awesome Word. We desperately need to cry out for the Holy Spirit to fill up all the dry areas of our lives and let God have His way with us once and for all.

However, we must not be like Jonah in the Old Testament. He was afraid to do what God asked of him, so he ran and jumped on a ship heading in the opposite direction. His running got him into a lot of trouble.

If we don't face our past, we cannot face our future. If we run from God and try to hide our past, we will never become free to be all that God is calling us to be.

A good example is when our builder came. He crawled under our house to check the original foundation. He wanted to assess the damage that could have happened in the past twenty-five years. He had to see if our older home could withstand a second story. He had to make sure there was no dry rot or leaky pipes that needed to be replaced before He could start the building project.

In our lives, we have to assess the damage that has been done because of our past. What have our lives been built upon? Do we have any source of bitterness or unforgiveness in our lives that could cause our foundation to be shaken? We must exchange our past and trust God with it. We must trust God in our daily lives and with our future, too.

Like Jonah, we, too, may try to run from our future. Jonah went through a big storm and got himself thrown into an enormous ocean. We, too, may find ourselves in a sea of despair. Jonah repented, and God spared his life, but it was after he had spent three days in the belly of a whale. I don't know about you, but I would rather face my past and future than run from them and get tossed around in the storms of life. When Jonah finally repented and obeyed God, he fulfilled his destiny by going to Nineveh.

Like Jonah, we must also repent and obey, before God can release us to fulfill our destiny. God will remove our sin and forgive us for running. God does care if we fail, He just forgives us when we ask. He wants to set us free from our past and for our hearts to obey His call upon our lives.

Disobedience leads to sin, which hurts God, others and eventually ourselves. It will hold you captive. Like Jonah, you might find yourself in a similar type of captivity. Healing must come to our past before God can do new things in our lives.

Despite the shame, God uses our past to bring Him glory. We become more compassionate toward others because we've walked in their shoes. We can give empathy instead of sympathy. When God heals your past and you are filled with Him, then His glory shines through you to others.

God used Jonah to preach to the people of Nineveh, and they repented. God spared them by passing no judgment upon them. God forgave Jonah and the people of Nineveh, and He forgives us. God doesn't seek to destroy us, but He wants to direct our lives lovingly, which can involve consequences and discipline.

In what areas of your life have you been withholding from God? Are you cheating on God and having a love affair with the world? The Word says in James 4:4 that if you are a friend of this world, you are an enemy to God. If we hold on to the areas of sin and shame in our lives, they become idols of distraction that will keep our eyes diverted from God.

An area of distraction in my life is when people wound me with what they say about me or how they perceive my actions negatively. This can heap so much shame on my life because it takes me back to the feelings of my past. An example is when I became "woman of the house" and my dad would offer a negative comment about how something was or wasn't done around the house. I thought, *If I could just do this good enough, then I would make my dad happy.* Well, it wasn't my job to make my dad happy with me. And still today, it's not my job to make people happy with me. But it is an area in my life that can keep me distracted enough that my eyes are on the situation, not on Jesus.

When we are dealing with our sin and shame, we need to understand the seriousness of it. Are we vying for control in some area of our lives? Do we have divided interests?

God is a jealous God. But as you come closer to God, He will draw nearer to you. God goes against the proud but gives grace to the humble. The areas of disloyalty in our lives must be cleansed. We must allow God to purify our inner life. We need to quit playing around with our past and hit rock bottom and cry out to God.

In my life, I need to get serious about exchanging my shame over how people feel about me. If I don't, I will continue to go around the same mountain again and again until I get sick and tired of it. I must stop listening in my mind to the shame people speak over me. Then I desperately need to replace this shame with what Jesus thinks about me.

As we get serious in our commitment to God, He will lift us up and replace our shame with more than we could hope or dream for. He will promote all of us in due time if we humble ourselves before Him.

But we must listen to what God is saying to us.

See to it that you do not refuse him who speaks. If they did not escape when they refused him who warned them on earth, how much less will we, if we turn away from him who warns us from heaven? At that time his voice shook the earth, but now he has promised, "Once more I will shake not only the earth but also the heavens.'" The words "once more" indicate the removing of what can be shaken—that is, created things—so that what cannot be shaken may remain. Therefore, since we are receiving a kingdom that cannot be shaken, let us be thankful, and so worship God acceptably with reverence and awe, for our God is a consuming fire.

—Hebrews 12:25–29, TLB

We must heed God's warning in our lives and obey His instructions. Don't be like the children of Israel. God is cleaning house and getting rid of your past. He won't quit until He is finished. He will sift out everything that has no solid foundation. Only His unshakable kingdom will be left standing.

Our foundations can be shaken if we are building our lives upon our past shame. If we exchange our pain and hurt for the healing power of Jesus, our foundation cannot be shaken.

God is the architect, and Jesus is the master builder. We cannot do this job by ourselves. Allow God to heal the foundation in your life. Let God call forth His original plan for your future. He wants to give you a fresh new life with new dreams and visions. Your past cannot disqualify you from God's plan and purposes in your life.

Take the time right now to ask God what areas in your life can shake your foundation or cause you to respond emotionally and withdraw from people and hold them at arm's length. What pain has caused you to become bitter and stunt your growth and shut down? Ask God to show you what holds you captive so He can release you from the bondage in your life. This is your opportunity to get free from your past.

Remember, we must tear down our foundation to rebuild. First Corinthians 15:36 says: "You foolish man! Every time you plant seed, you sow something that does not come to life [germinating, springing up, and growing] unless it dies first" (AMP). Therefore, we must die to our flesh and our old way of doing things before we can experience God's presence and glory in our lives. Verses 42 and 43 say, "So it is with the resurrection of the dead. [The body] that is sown is perishable and decays, but [the body] that is resurrected is imperishable (immune to decay, immortal). It is sown in dishonor and humiliation; it is raised in honor *and* glory. It is sown in infirmity *and* weakness; it is resurrected in strength *and* endued with power" (AMP).

No matter what we or others have done to cause dishonor in our lives, God will raise us up in His honor and glory. The sick, weak areas of our lives will be resurrected in strength, and we will be given His power. When we give up our old ways, our hurts, our shame and our past, Jesus will give us new life by His resurrected power, and we will become imperishable and unshakable.

But we have to *choose* this path. Jesus will never force His will upon our lives. He is a complete gentleman. We are the ones who decide what shame we are ready to deal with and surrender to Him. Until you are ready to move on, it is okay to stay right where you are.

Jesus will never put overwhelming pressure on your life to change. He will, however, gently nudge at these areas and encourage you to make your shame exchanges. He knows how you feel. He just wants to see you free.

Once you have changed, you should never go back to the past unless it is for healing purposes. We need to continue to press forward and leave our past behind so we can be all Jesus wants us to be, and to run the race to which we've been called until we see His face.

Our past pain then becomes useful. God doesn't waste it; He uses it to develop His character in us. It becomes part of our life message. So don't be afraid to share your pain so other people can be free from their shame.

As we change, our lives are transformed into His image. God gives us the victory and makes us more than conquerors. First Corinthians 15:58 says, "Therefore, my beloved brethren, be firm (steadfast), immovable, always abounding in the work of the Lord [always being superior, excelling, doing more than enough in the service of the Lord], knowing *and* being continually aware that your labor in the Lord is not futile [it is never wasted or to no purpose]" (AMP). Be firm and stand on the unshakable rock: Jesus. Be immovable and unshakable and live in His Glory.

We need to rejoice and be thankful that we get to share in Christ's suffering. We are in a refining process with God's glory waiting for us just around the bend. As we worship God with a deep reverence, we will experience God's glory in our lives. And as we experience God's glory, our lives will begin to change.

> Dear friends, don't be bewildered or surprised when you go through the fiery trials ahead, for this is no strange, unusual thing that is going to happen to you. Instead, be really glad—because these trials will make you partners with Christ in his suffering, and afterwards you will have the wonderful joy of sharing his glory in that coming day when it will be displayed.
>
> —1 PETER 4:12–13, TLB

What exactly is this glory we will experience?

I like what Ruth Ward Heflin said in *Glory: Experiencing the Atmosphere of Heaven* about God's glory:

"When glory comes down, it's a bit of heaven's atmosphere coming down to us, a taste of His manifest presence. We don't see the air we breathe—but we would be dead if we didn't breathe it. We're not conscious of the air unless we see the wind moving the leaves on a tree. The earth is covered by it. Not one inch of heaven lacks glory." That is awesome to think about. Not one inch of heaven lacks God's glory.

The Greek definition of *glory* is "the manifest presence of God." It means "splendor, brightness, majesty of God." John Bevere's definition of glory in his book *A Heart Ablaze* states, "The glory of the Lord is everything that makes God, God. All His characteristics, authority, power, and wisdom. Literally, the immeasurable weight and magnitude of God." We are to be the radiance of God revealing His glory through us.

Man was made to be a reflection of God's glory. As people recognize God in us, we are reflecting God's glory.

> But we Christians have no veil over our faces; we can be mirrors that brightly reflect the glory of the Lord. As the Spirit of the Lord works within us, we become more and more like him.
> —2 Corinthians 3:18, TLB

A reflection of God's glory is much like a reflection we might see in a beautiful pond. My home is next to a pond, and at the right time of day, you can see the farmhouse reflecting off the water. That reflection can be breathtaking.

That is exactly how we reflect the image of our heavenly Father. When we stand under His shadow, we reflect

His image and we are attractive to the people we meet. If we get out from underneath His shadow, we won't reflect His image; we'll reflect our own.

Under the shadow of the Almighty God is a safe place to stand. If we stand anywhere else, we will be uncovered and unprotected from the attacks that come into our everyday lives.

The more we fall in love with Jesus, the more we become like Him. And the more we will experience His unending glory. We are increasing from one degree of glory to another. Let His glory break the chains of shame that bind us so tightly and set every captive free from all effects of sin and shame.

Are you ready to take the challenge and be a vessel that brightly reflects His glory?

Please take the time right now to pray this prayer with me:

> *Dear Jesus, I give You every ounce of me—all my sin, all my shame, all my hurts and pain. I will no longer withhold any part of my life from You. I surrender all my life to You. I need You to heal my past and set this captive free. Thank You, Lord, for replacing my shame with Your glory.*

SEVEN

The Power of His Glory Breaks Shame

A few years ago, I was in a church service one evening, and the pastor began saying that many people were brokenhearted. I felt an urge to step out of my seat and move toward the front, where many people were already being prayed over. As I moved out of my comfort zone and walked down to the altar, it felt like a wave hit my emotions, and I began to weep uncontrollably. I had no idea why God wanted me to be prayed over, and I had no idea why I was so broken. I just wanted to obey the nudging I felt in my heart and be open to God healing my brokenness.

As God began to speak to me, I felt Him whisper in my ear that I was broken over my family. He was telling me that my family's hurt and pain wasn't my burden to carry; it was His. Jesus was the One who brought salvation and healing into my life, and I needed to release my family's deepest hurts to Him.

As I began to lift this burden up to the Lord, I felt a load lift from my shoulders. Complete peace took over, and the weeping stopped. Now, not even I stood between my family and the Lord.

After I was prayed over, I went back to my seat, where a woman whispered in my ear, "Isaiah 61." I was familiar with that scripture, but I had no idea how much God would use it to transform my life over the years ahead.

Isaiah 61 starts out proclaiming, "The Spirit of the Lord God is upon me, because the Lord has anointed me to bring good news to the suffering and afflicted. He has sent me to comfort the brokenhearted, to announce liberty to captives and to open the eyes of the blind. He has sent me to tell those who mourn that the time of God's favor to them has come, and the day of his wrath to their enemies. To all who mourn in Israel he will give: Beauty for ashes; joy instead of mourning; praise instead of heaviness. For God has planted them like strong and graceful oaks for His own glory" (TLB).

I believe this scripture is a prophetic word over my personal life and perhaps over yours also. These verses show what we can exchange our shame for. For example, if we trade in our heaviness, God will replace it with praise. Our mourning will turn into joy, and our ashes will be exchanged for beauty.

Just as Jesus has set me free in many areas of my life, I long for Him to set every captive of shame free.

Many of us are in family situations that are less than

perfect. I would say all of us would be lying if we said our lives were perfect and complete. But as I've gotten older, I've come to realize I don't have to believe the lie that I must be perfect.

Too many of us want so badly to reflect God's image that we think we must reflect perfection to do this. This is a lie from the enemy. If we are honest and unashamed before Christ, we can be vulnerable with our lives before others. I know people love it when I share my testimony. It causes them to relax and see me as a real person, not just someone who is in front of the church leading people in worship.

It's time for us to exchange this way of thinking for God's way of thinking. He doesn't expect perfection! He does, however, expect our best. A friend shared this motto with me one day long ago, and it has stayed with me: "Give God your best, and then let Him do the rest." I believe this is so true. Sometimes to God, my best looks different than it does to the world. This is fine, because what He thinks is what sets me free. Worrying about what the world thinks about me will only hold me captive.

As I began to recognize how hard I was trying to make everyone in my family happy, I realized it was probably the very thing that was driving them from me. I just wanted them to like me, and so I tried hard to please them in any way I could.

Sometimes when we don't trust the Lord, we try to take the bull by the horns and do things the way we think they should be done. To our surprise, most of the time, the Lord's way of doing things is quite different from ours. If we would just get out of the way, then the Lord could begin to work.

Oftentimes, we can block what the Lord is trying to

do because we flat out try too hard. We try to make everybody happy. We try to please this person or that person. We don't want to make waves, so we try so hard to do and say the right things. But in the end, we are usually the ones who end up feeling miserable and exhausted. This is not our job.

This is exactly what brought me down. I was feeling shame because I couldn't meet everybody's needs and I couldn't make everyone happy. I felt I needed to say and do the right things so they would love me and accept me. But I soon found out my efforts to be perfect always resulted in disaster. I always left feeling shame because I couldn't please everyone all the time.

A good example of this was during the holidays before my dad died. Mark and I would be on a roller coaster ride during the Christmas season. We would have Christmas at my mom's house two weeks before Christmas, and then go back and have Christmas with my dad on Christmas Eve. Then we would leave late that night and travel two and a half hours to get home to have Christmas with Mark's family on Christmas day. Most of the time, I ended up feeling tired, lonely and worn out by the time all these celebrations were over. My heart was to honor everyone, but I always ended up disappointing someone in the process. I would think, *How can we keep going on like this? We certainly can't keep doing this, especially when we have children.*

This shame I was feeling came from Satan, not from God. He tries to get all of us to believe that something is wrong with who we are, that no matter what we say or do, we will never measure up to people's expectations of us. We can try as hard as we can to meet everyone's needs, but we'll always come up short. Then when we return home, the shame we experience leaves us feeling as if we don't belong and that we will never fit in.

We must realize we cannot make people ultimately happy. Certainly, we can bring joy to someone's life or cause someone to experience love by our actions, but only God's love can truly fill people's emptiness. People will always let us down or disappoint us in some way. That doesn't mean we quit trying in our relationships, but it does mean we need to surrender them to Jesus so He can ultimately meet their deepest longings.

Anyone dealing with divorce or death can relate to how I was feeling. I would feel deep shame because I knew I had let someone down.

Then somewhere in this wild ride of my life, I remembered that Jesus was nailed to the cross to bear my sin and shame. God's heart for me was to take all the burdens and heaviness away from my life. I needed to exchange this shame and be released to be Laurie, who has real feelings and needs of her own.

Luke talks about the two men who were nailed to the cross on both sides of Jesus. One of the criminals said, "So you're the Messiah, are You? Prove it by saving yourself and us, too, while you're at it!" But the other criminal protested. "Don't you even fear God when you are dying? We deserve to die for our evil deeds, but this man hasn't done one thing wrong." Then he said, "Jesus, remember me when you come into your Kingdom." And Jesus replied, "Today you will be with me in Paradise. This is a solemn promise" (Luke 23:39–43, TLB).

Jesus wants to free us from our sin and shame just like this criminal on the cross. All of us need to realize that we deserved to die, and when we choose to repent and love the Lord, He begins the process of setting us free from our sin and shame.

When we give our lives to Jesus, He will release us from our shame and forgive us for our sins. When we get to heaven, the One who will be carrying our sin and shame will be Jesus. He will carry all the scars from our lives, and we will be spotless and blameless before Him. Jesus wants us to take our sin and shame and nail it to the cross one last time.

Quit dwelling on the past and focus on the future that God has called us to share: eternity with Him and His Son. If we can have a perspective change, we can rise above all our pain and emotions and move on. But if we choose to carry our shame, we will try to hide it from the Lord and everyone else—just as Adam and Eve did after they ate from the fruit that God told them not to touch. They hid from the Lord because they recognized their nakedness, and they became ashamed. We cannot hide from the Lord. He already knows everything about us. When we hide, it hurts us and others around us. It also hurts the Lord. If we understand the fear of the Lord, we would not withhold one thing from Him. The Bible says, "The fear of the LORD is the beginning of wisdom" (Ps. 111:10, NKJV). John Bevere shares in his book *The Fear of the Lord*, "Holy fear gives God the place of glory, honor, reverence, thanksgiving, praise and pre-eminence He deserves." (Notice it is *what* He deserves, not what we *think* He deserves.)

If we understand how awesome God is, we will never want to hide our shame because of His deep love for us. He knows how deeply we hurt, and it causes Him pain when we don't exchange our shame. We need to run to the Lord instead of hiding. He is the only One who can cleanse us and set us free.

Shame has a tendency to make you shrink from the Lord and withdraw from people. Many times in my life, I have had this happen because the pull to return to my past was so strong. It is comfortable there, and I know just how to cope with my feelings and emotions. I could run and hide and not face the shame or deal with the pain. Oftentimes when people were involved, I would avoid them altogether, or at least hold them at arm's length. Does this behavior sound familiar to you? We all tend to return to the familiar, especially when the heat is on in our relationship with other people. We all have coping mechanisms we like to fall back on.

One example in my life is when I was in a close friendship and some things were said that really wounded my spirit. Little did this person know that anytime someone raised his voice at me it took me back subconsciously to a time when my dad yelled at me for something that was out of my control. Instead of wanting to fix this issue, I went home and soaked in my bathtub and cried. Over a period of days, I didn't want to deal with this person because I was hurt and offended. What I didn't know was that the longer I held the offense, the more time the enemy had to work to destroy this relationship.

Now I know that if I don't deal with the pain, it blocks my relationship with God, which in turn stunts my growth. I'm stuck again until I decide to fix the broken record that keeps playing over and over again in my mind.

Why are we so afraid to face our fears and confront our pain? What fear keeps us in the grips of shame? One way to fix this broken record in our lives is to endure the pain of our shame and walk through it for as long as it takes to get free.

We have all felt shame at one time or another. We have felt humiliated, and we never want to see the people who brought it on us again. Sometimes shame comes from what we have done or said. Other times, shame comes from people who have hurt us verbally, physically or emotionally.

Those are the unjust situations in our lives. When my parents divorced, things got out of my control very quickly. I couldn't change the situation at home or stop my parents from divorcing. Our lives can get out of our control when we are wounded by people—usually those who love us the most.

What area in your life feels out of control because of wounds you've experienced either as a child or as an adult?

Let me share with you a story that left me and my family feeling out of control. It happened after my niece Cassidy was killed. This devastating loss made life stand still for my family. We were frozen emotionally, wondering how we could survive the pain of this loss.

Cassidy was thirteen when she died. Months prior to her death, she came to spend some time with me. I had the privilege of taking Cass to lunch and shopping for a new dress. As we visited during lunch, I learned that her mom and dad were not doing well in their marriage. I looked Cassidy in the eyes and vowed to her, "I don't care if your parents never speak to me again, I will fight for their marriage."

At that moment, I never could have known the battle that was to come. But I will never regret making that promise to her.

That same year, the day after Christmas, Cassidy and her friend were walking on a sidewalk by a high school. A young man pulled out of the school parking lot and reached down to pick up a cassette off his floorboard. His car jumped the curb. It hit Cassidy first, killing her instantly. Her friend was taken to the intensive care unit with external injuries.

When I got the phone call notifying me of her death, time stood still. If you have ever had someone close to you die an untimely death, you know what I am talking about. I didn't know if I should scream or cry. My instincts were to be with my brother and his family, so Mark and I hopped in our car and made the long drive to my brother's house.

On the way there, we prayed as we had never prayed before. I cried out to God, "How will my family ever be able to bear this pain of losing a child?" I kept putting myself in my brother's place. I thought, *How could I ever withstand the pain of losing one of my children?* This pain was so raw and so real. There was nothing more I could do but be there for my family. It was a helpless feeling.

As a family, we went through the motions during the days preceding the memorial service. At Cassidy's service, hundreds of people from this small community came to show their support. Only a tragic death like this can stop a town from functioning. Life seemed to stand still for all those whose lives were touched by my young niece.

None of us could have foreseen this coming. My brother, sister-in-law and their other two daughters were overcome with grief. *How could any of us help them through this incredibly hard time?* Once again, I knew the only thing I had to give them was the love and grace found in Jesus.

As the days and months went by, my sweet sister-in-law began to close down and withdraw from her family and most of her friends. I instinctively knew something was wrong. Soon she moved out and ran from her family. She just couldn't handle the pain because there was so much shame involved. Some of you may be wondering, How can there be shame involved in death? Death is final, and all the things you wished you would have said or done can no longer be said or done.

All my brother's and sister-in-law's hopes and dreams for their daughter would not come to pass on this earth. They were left trying to measure her life with eternal value, and that is hard for the ones left on earth to deal with.

Of course, my brother and their other daughters were even more devastated when my sister-in-law left. She was the type of mom anyone would love to call their own. She was their all in all. Perhaps in Cindy's own hidden shame of her past lay the reasons for her trying to be the "perfect mom and wife." No one can be perfect, and I know Cindy felt so much failure as a mother when her youngest daughter died. Of course, as it was with me, this was all a lie from the enemy. But no one could persuade her of this during her time of deep grief.

Looking back at that time, I remembered my vow to Cassidy. I promised her that I would fight for her parents' marriage, and that is what I intended to do. I would keep my promise by running a marathon while praying for Cassidy's parents the entire distance.

If you have ever run a marathon, you understand how much training is involved. It takes miles and miles of running to build up your body so you can withstand the 26.2–mile race. I remember feeling impressed by God that it would take a marathon of prayer to see Him heal their marriage. I set out and prayed to God with every step I took. Whether I ran or walked, I prayed. Mile after mile, prayer after prayer, I cried out to the Lord. I wasn't prepared for the emotions that would overcome me. It was like I was living my young life all over again. As I ran and prayed for my brother's marriage, the raw emotions of my own parents' divorce came up again. It felt as if I were standing in the gap for Cassidy; I could feel the pain of a broken marriage and how it affected my life. This marathon of prayer was costly for me, not only physically, but emotionally as well. But it was a great outlet for me, to run every day and intercede for my family.

In the meantime, I encouraged my brother to start running and praying. I knew it would be good for his emotions and his health. He had too much time on his hands to dwell on his deep loss and pain. I wanted to see him shift that pain to produce spiritual health in his life. I knew that he, too, needed to take a stand and cry out to God for his family. Together we were holding onto the ground that the enemy was trying to steal from him.

What happened over the next several months took us all by surprise. My brother had reached a point of desperation. He had hit rock bottom emotionally, physically and spiritually. He had no more resources from which to pull. He was done fighting for his marriage, so he finally released his wife and family completely to God. He told God, with tears streaming down his face, that if his wife didn't ever come back to him, she was His. He said, "I will always love her, but I surrender her to You."

Two weeks later, on Father's Day, my sister-in-law came home and repented to my brother and my nieces. When

Fred called me later that day, he asked me to sit down. First, fear ran through my mind as I wondered, *What could have happened?* We did the dance of joy as we wept over his wife's return. It was a moment we'll never forget.

That was in late June, and it wasn't until late September that I would run the marathon. I knew they would still need lots of prayer, so I continued to train for my race.

At the starting line the morning of the race, with minutes to go before the gun went off, Cindy came over and asked me, "Why are you running this race?" With tears in my eyes, I shared with her my promise to Cassidy. I had told my brother about it months earlier, but my sister-in-law only knew a little bit of the story. We both wept so hard that I knew I would never leave the starting line unless the gun went off soon. After a huge embrace, Cindy went to the sidewalk, and I started the race.

Mile after mile, when I saw my brother's face and heard my sister-in-law's shouts of encouragement, I would almost weep uncontrollably at what God had done for their marriage. Many times, I would cry so hard I would begin to labor in my breathing. I knew that if I wanted to finish this race for Cassidy, I had to keep my emotions under control.

At about mile thirteen, the toughest part of the course, I remember feeling so strong that I felt like I was flying for miles. I couldn't feel my feet hit the pavement, and I didn't feel the impact of all the miles I had run. It was an incredible feeling.

The last several miles, my brother ran with me. Mile after mile, he kept telling me, "Laurie, look what God has done." I kept crying and telling him to be quiet so I could finish the race. As we approached the finish line, my brother leaned over and kissed me on the cheek and told me he loved me. Sobbing deeply, I finished the race I had promised to run for Cassidy.

As I write this story, I have tears streaming down my face. I could never explain how it feels to understand that my God answers prayers—even in the most unjust situations.

> For I, the Lord, love justice; I hate robbery and wrong. I will faithfully reward my people for their suffering and make an everlasting covenant with them.
>
> —Isaiah 61:8, TLB

Losing my niece still feels like such an injustice. As a family, we may never understand all the whys about Cassidy's death, but we do understand that God is close to those whose hearts are breaking. We also will never forget the miracle that took place in my brother's marriage and family all because of a promise that had to be kept for a young girl named Cassidy LeeAnne Rose.

If there is an area in your life where you feel out of control, I encourage you to surrender everything to the Lord as soon as possible. Just as He did when my brother surrendered his wife, God is waiting to take the unjust situations in your life and make them just. I know He wants to pour out His mercy and blessings on those who have suffered great injustice. He wants to give you a double portion of His glory in all your areas of hurt and shame.

When we make mistakes, although we get to learn and grow from our wrong choices, we sometimes will suffer the consequences. When we suffer because of what others have said or done, God is broken, and in His mercy, He will reward those who suffer because of injustice.

Isn't that a great deal? By letting Jesus have all our shame, it is replaced with His amazing glory. The glory of the Lord will rest on our lives, and that will get people's attention. When Jesus walked on this earth, He was manifesting the presence of God wherever He went. Jesus reflected God's glory to the world. Wherever Jesus went, lives were changed and touched.

> My prayer for all of them is that they will be of one heart and mind, just as you and I are, Father—that just as you are in me and I am in you, so they will be in us, and the world will believe you sent me. I have given them the glory you gave me—the glorious unity of being one, as we are—I in them and you in me, all being perfected into one—so that the world will know you sent me and will understand that you love them as much as you love me. Father, I want them with me—these you've given me—so that they can see my glory. You gave me the glory because you loved me before the world began!
>
> —JOHN 17:21–24, TLB

One of the ways God's glory can shine the brightest in our lives is by us walking in unity with God and other people around us. We can usher in the glory of God by practicing oneness. When we love God with all our heart, soul and mind, then we can love our neighbors as ourselves.

How many of us are really loving our neighbors as we love ourselves? Are we really laying down our lives for others instead of pleasing ourselves? The healing power of God's glory can fall in our lives more powerfully when we walk with Him in unity and when we walk in that same unity with our brothers and sisters in Christ.

An example of God replacing shame with His amazing glory lies in the history of my church. When our church split years ago, the names of the church, the school, the pastor and his family were dragged through the mud because of differences in opinion. There was so much shame spoken over my pastor and his family. I couldn't believe the severity of the lies.

For about a year, those of us left in our church were afraid to be vulnerable to one another because we were so protective of our lives. We were sure that if we shared our hearts with anyone, it would turn into gossip and be spread viciously across town.

There is nothing the devil loves more than to cause a pastor and a church to walk in shame. That's because shame keeps you self-centered and ineffective for the kingdom of God and in the lives of those around you. Shame causes you to hang your head and hide. It causes you to guard your heart and not share it with anyone so you won't get hurt again.

As our church walked through this pain of shame and dishonor spoken about us, God started to peel off the layers of shame so that we could bear fruit again.

The peeling process was like removing layers of wallpaper. The first layer comes off easily, but the second and third layers require much work. You must soak the paper then size it and let it rest before you can begin peeling off the paper. It will come off in small strips, but when the effort is over, you have a nice, clean wall.

This is a good example of what I felt God was doing in our church. He was pulling back the layers of hurt and shame so we could be free again. The first layer came off easily, but there were deeper areas that took lots of extra work in our hearts to remove. This came through deep repentance and forgiveness. I will never forget the day my pastor repented in tears for his part in the disunity that caused the church to split. He was so broken and visibly shaken. But it changed the direction of our church. I have enduring respect for my pastor because of his ability to be humble enough to repent.

This process has gone on for years, but as the shame fell off, God's glory could then fall. For the last several years, I have been praying for this.

One way God has replaced the shame and dishonor that was spoken about our church with His glory is by giving us incredible relationships with churches across the United States and worldwide. We have formed an alliance with these churches, and we now pray for and act as a covering for their ministries. They come to my pastor for help and advice, and we can call the alliance when we need help, prayer or advice. Because of this alliance, we have friendships and relationships with people in many different states and countries, such as, Oregon, Arizona, New York, New Jersey, Texas, Cuba, Russia, Azerbaijan, India, Mexico, Guatemala and Nicaragua.

The leaders in the alliance include Wilson Nease, Dr. Negiel Bigpond, Bishop Ezra N. Williams, Rev. Gordon E. Williams and Rev. Carlton T. Brown and Pastor Jon Bowers.

We have a special relationship with Pastor Augustus Anthony ("Pastor Tony"), who is vital to the alliance, and his family from India. There are so many more people I could list here. At the time of this writing, we had just held our third pastor conference when all nine churches we cover came together for one glorious week.

Picture eighty-nine people from Harlem flying into Oregon to be part of this conference. Did God's glory ever show up! We took sixty-one pastors and their wives on a jet boat trip, and we had the time of our lives. When we finished the two-hour trip, the driver said that in his eleven years of jet boat driving, he had never seen such happy people. We were reflecting God's glory, even on the boat trip.

Picture Caucasian, African-American and Spanish people loving on each other and laughing until their sides hurt.

Wherever we went, God's glory rested. We ate at a restaurant, and the owner found out who we were and what we were about. When you take sixty-one pastors and their wives anywhere, people take notice. The restaurant owner said we could set up our sound system in her restaurant and minister there during business hours.

One pastor shared his testimony of how he had put ministry before his wife and family and even before his relationship with God. He explained that building a ministry was everything to him, and his family had suffered to the point that it was almost destroyed. Then God got hold of this pastor and sent him to our church to walk through our restoration ministry. He saw how he was not loving his family as he loved himself and the growth of his ministry. God restored his marriage and his ministry, and this pastor wanted to give God all the glory.

As he was sharing this, a man from the restaurant shared, in tears, how his wife wanted a divorce after twenty-five years of marriage. This man got saved right there because of a pastor sharing his testimony and God's healing power touching lives through others. After this man got saved, he said he had never seen such "happy-faced people in all of his life."

Can you image the glory that filled that place because of the different races that were walking together in unity, with the same purpose, same heart, and same mind? That is oneness at its best.

God is looking for something great to happen through all of us. It's not about who we are; it's about who we are in Christ. When we brag on what Jesus has done in our lives, He should get all the glory and honor.

Humble yourself and stay out of God's way. Have a willingness to surrender everything, even your past, to the Lord.

Humble yourself and stay out of God's way.

God may have you right where He wants you...broken. When you are broken, God has your full attention because you have nowhere else to go. Nothing you can do will change your circumstances. Let God have His way with you, and then His glory can fall in your life, just as it did in my pastor's life. He was broken, but he let God have His way with him, his family and his ministry, and the results were a double portion coming from all over the world.

For God to heal you, not only do you have to be humble, but you also have to hear from Him. This means getting quiet enough in our lives to do this. Sometimes God has to humble us so we will hear Him.

He humbled this pastor and his ministry, who heard and obeyed. Only then could he and his family be healed.

Many of us want to rush off to others to fill the emptiness in our lives. We want others to heal our broken lives and fix our problems. We want the quickest solutions with as little pain involved as possible. We're often so full of ourselves that there is no room for Jesus to come in and heal us.

With God's glory, you don't need anyone or anything else to help you experience His touch. All you need is Him. In Exodus 33:18, Moses cries out to God, "I beseech You, show me Your glory" (AMP).

My heart's cry for His glory is written in this song:

> *Show me Your glory, I want to see Your face.*
> *Show me Your glory, I long for Your embrace.*
> *I'm hungry for You. I'm desperate for You.*
> *We cry out for Your presence.*
> *We cry out for Your presence.*
> *We cry out for the presence of the Lord.*
> —LAURIE SMUCKER (2001)

I have learned over the years that people can and will disappoint me and let me down. They will fail me at times and not be there when I need them to be. My only source of encouragement is that Jesus is always available, day or night, at any second.

Here is an example of God showing up when I least expected it. One morning, as I was preparing for the day, I went through the usual process of showering, brushing my teeth, fixing my hair and putting on my make-up so I would be presentable for the chapel service I would speak at later that morning. I wasn't expecting to hear from God that morning, but nonetheless He spoke to me.

I put my Bible down on the folding table in my laundry room and gazed out the window. What stopped me from rushing around was the sun shining off the creek that runs by our house. I paused for a moment, and this is what God impressed in my spirit: "Glory is like the morning sun shimmering off a lake. Glory is like a warm summer breeze brushing by your face. Glory is like the warmth of the sun's rays penetrating deep within. Glory is a touch from heaven, which can be unspeakable, unfathomable, indescribable and undeniable." I just stood there and gazed out the window. I felt an urge to go out on the porch and just breathe in the fresh morning air. As I went outside, a song rose from my heart as I experienced the glory of God right on my back porch. It took my breath away as I relaxed and felt embraced in the warm morning sun.

Glory is awesome. Pause right now and ponder His glory. Jesus says, "Dwell in me, and I will dwell in you. Live in Me, and I will live in you. Abide in My love, and My love will abide in you." (See John 15.) Let God reveal Himself to you at this moment.

I do this with my children by playing a game as we lie on our trampoline outside. Most of the time, we have jumped until I cannot jump anymore, so I invented this game to catch my breath. They can always keep jumping. I'll get them to lie still long enough to close their eyes and listen. After several moments have passed, I'll ask them, "What do you hear?" They might respond, "Mom, I hear the birds chirping," or, "Mom, I hear the wind rustling in the leaves." "Mom, I hear the crickets creaking," or, "Mom, I hear the frogs croaking." "Mom, I hear the sounds of a car passing by," or, "Mom, I hear the loud engine of a tractor going by." This game can go on and on until they can no longer lie still. I love our fun moments on the trampoline. Those memories will last a lifetime.

God's glory is all over the place. All we have to do is slow down and surrender to His presence.

God's glory is all over the place. All we have to do is slow down and surrender to His presence. Then we will experience the manifest presence of God in all we see, do and hear.

What are we going to do to usher in God's glory on this earth? In our everyday lives, God's glory is changing us to become more like Him. Let Him heal your broken heart. Let Him set you free.

> To all who mourn in Israel he will give:
>> Beauty for ashes;
>> Joy instead of mourning;
>> Praise instead of a spirit of heaviness.
>
> For God has planted them like strong and graceful oaks for his own glory.... You shall be called priests of the Lord, ministers of our God.... Instead of shame and dishonor, you shall have a double portion of prosperity and everlasting joy. For I, the Lord, love justice; I hate robbery and wrong. I will faithfully reward my people for their suffering and make an everlasting covenant with them. Their descendants shall be known and honored among the nations; all shall realize that they are a people God has blessed. Let me tell you how happy God has made me! For he has clothed me with garments of salvation and draped about me the robe of righteousness. I am like a bridegroom in his wedding suit or a bride with her jewels. The Lord will show the

nations of the world his justice; all will praise him.
His righteousness shall be like a budding tree, or like
a garden in early spring, full of young plants
springing up everywhere.

—ISAIAH 61:3, 6–11, TLB

Don't you love the promises of God? Rest in those
promises and run the race.

SOMETHING TO THINK ABOUT

- Give a personal definition of shame.

- Who bore our sin and shame?

- When we try to hide, whom does it hurt most?

- List some areas of shame in your life and
  where you think they come from.

- What does Isaiah 61:8 say the Lord will do
  with our shame?

- When Jesus takes our shame, with what does
  He replace it?

- John 17:21–24 shares about Jesus and the
  Father being One. Does He want this kind of
  oneness for all of us?

- When does God's glory shine the brightest in
  our lives?

- Name the three areas in our lives in which we
  need God's glory to rest.

- What will you do to usher in God's glory on
  this earth?

EIGHT

A New Name:
World-Changers

When God comes first in our lives, we aren't the only ones who can abound in His glory. Thanks to our relationship with Jesus, the lives of those around us can change forever.

In my daily life, I am busy keeping up with my children, running back and forth to sporting events, school functions or church services. Often during my busy times, I am nudged to pray for someone in particular. When God does this, I know my obedience could possibly change someone's world on any given day.

You may be wondering, *How could I change someone's world?* The answer is simple: Pray and obey!

On one particular day, I couldn't get a young friend

named Jennifer off my mind. I kept asking God what it was He wanted me to do. He just encouraged me to visit her. I figured I better obey because the nudging wasn't going away. As I dropped by her house, I found a young woman who was distraught emotionally after a break-up in a relationship. After I listened for some time, I told Jennifer the only thing I had to offer her was Jesus, and if she wanted to share more to come by my house later. I was giving her some time to think, to see if she was ready to receive Jesus as Lord of her life. Several hours later, she came by.

I was sitting on my couch listening to her share about her pain, and the tears started to pour down her face. She was emotionally, physically and spiritually exhausted. I had been praying during this time, and I knew I had only one thing to give her—the greatest gift of all, the gift of salvation. I simply asked her if she wanted to give all her pain and disappointment to Jesus. I told her Jesus was the One who loved her more than anyone else could, and He was the only One who could meet her deepest longing. With great honor, I took Jennifer's hand that day as she prayed with me to accept Jesus into her heart for the first time. At that moment, she understood that Jesus bore all her sin, shame and pain, and in exchange, she would receive a fresh, new start on life. She now felt the peace and hope that comes into a person's life after making Jesus Lord of her life.

Jennifer received a name change at that moment. It wasn't a literal name change, but Jennifer's "identity" had changed. At this moment, she was a daughter of the King of kings. Jennifer was now a born-again Christian. The apostle Peter describes this transformation as being "priests of the King…holy and pure…God's very own"

(1 Pet. 2:9, TLB). Jennifer's life will now reflect to others how God has called her out of the darkness and into His wonderful light. Once Jennifer was less than nothing; now she is God's very own. Once she knew little of God's kindness; now her life has been changed by it.

Perhaps for the first time in Jennifer's life, she had a purpose, a hope, and a bright new future. She had been adopted into God's family, and everything was beginning to take on new light. Her face glowed, and she wore a big smile. No longer did the burdens she had been carrying affect her. She had exchanged them for the joy of the Lord, which was now evident in her life.

All heaven was rejoicing over this new child of God. After Jennifer left, I wanted to leap for joy. I was overwhelmed with the fact that God had used me to bring salvation to one of His lost lambs. At that moment, I started to give thanks and praise to God not only for Jennifer's salvation, but for mine.

I am so glad I obeyed the nudging of the Lord that day. If I had kept moving that day and ignored what God was saying to me, I would have missed an opportunity to change someone's world by leading her to Jesus.

This is how God uses ordinary people to do extraordinary things. If we are available to listen to His voice and then obey Him when He tells us exactly what to do, we get the great privilege of changing someone's life for all eternity.

The Book of Isaiah talks about receiving a new name.

> The nations shall see your righteousness. Kings shall be blinded by your glory; and God will confer on you a new name. He will hold you aloft in his hands for all to see—a splendid crown for the King of kings.

Never again shall you be called 'The God-forsaken
Land' or the 'Land that God Forgot.' Your new
name will be 'The Land of God's Delight' and 'The
Bride,' for the Lord delights in you and will claim
you as His own"

—Isaiah 62:2–4, TLB

Because of God's deep, enduring love for each of us,
He promises us a name in which He can delight. We are
the Bride of Christ, and we can have no deeper relationship. God views us as whole, spotless and blameless.

When God's glory has replaced the shame in our lives,
we receive a new identity. No longer will shame and dishonor affect us the way it used to. We will recognize
shame when it comes, but we will not allow Satan to use it
to keep us stuck in our past or cause us to be ineffective in
our lives any longer.

I love knowing that even when we think our gifts are
small, God promises He will use them. I love knowing I
cannot do anything to make Jesus love me one ounce
more. I rejoice in knowing there is nothing in my past
that could make Him close the door on me.

All He asks is that we continually come to the Father.
Be alert to God's prompting. He may want to use you to
change someone's world, maybe even today.

As we do this, it is important to remember where we
came from and who brought wholeness into our lives. We
all need Jesus as Lord of every area of our lives. In our
daily lives, we must constantly come back to our heavenly
Father and fill up again. If we try to give His love, His
grace and His glory away by ourselves, we will fall flat on
our faces. It is only through what He has done that we can
even stand today.

When we are given a new name, there will be many times when God will ask us to give out in ministry. When God's healing power is at work in our lives and He wants us to share our lives with others so they may be healed, this is our "life message." God fills us up so He can pour out His love through us, and we get to give His love away.

The Bible contains many examples of God giving a new name to someone. For instance, in Genesis 32:24–28, Jacob wrestled all night to be blessed with a new name.

Throughout Jacob's life, he had not been an honest man. An example of his dishonesty is found in Genesis 27. Jacob was the one who tricked his brother Esau out of his rightful blessing from their father, Isaac. Even though Jacob got his father's blessing, it cost him dearly. He had to flee from his family because his brother wanted to kill him, plus he never got to see his mother again. He was then deceived by his own uncle Laban over his wife, and he had to live with the fact that his family was torn apart because of his selfish actions. And yet we find out that something had later changed so much in Jacob's heart that he was willing to wrestle all night for a name change.

Jacob had been wrestling with his past. He desperately wanted to leave it behind and make things right with Esau. In fact, Jacob had made the first move and sent word to his brother that he was coming to greet him. However, a message was returned to Jacob that Esau was on his way to meet him with an army of four hundred men. I'm sure Jacob was now desperate and frantic and afraid. Can you imagine, your brother whom you betrayed is coming to meet you with an army? Jacob had nothing left to do but cry out to God in prayer.

Many times in our lives, we are as desperate as Jacob,

and all we can do is cry out to God in prayer. We, too, have changed, but like Jacob, how will anyone ever believe us?

Jacob spent the night crying out to God and declaring His promises. He hadn't seen his brother for twenty years, so Jacob also was preparing a gift for Esau to try to appease him before they met face-to-face. During the night, Jacob had a surprise encounter with an angel, and he wrestled all night for the blessings of the Lord upon his life.

> Then He said, Let me go, for day is breaking. But *Jacob* said, I will not let You go unless You declare a blessing upon me. [The Man] asked him, What is your name? And [in shock of realization, whispering] he said, Jacob [supplanter, schemer, trickster, swindler]! And He said, Your name shall be called no more Jacob [supplanter], but Israel [contender with God]; for you have contended and have power with God and with men and have prevailed.
>
> —GENESIS 32:26–28, AMP

Jacob had changed. Can you imagine the softening of character that took place this night in Jacob's life? He had prevailed, and now he had the courage to humbly go and meet his brother in peace. He no longer felt fear, only a deep sense of contentment and anticipation of what God was going to do to restore his relationship with his brother.

Far off in a distance, Jacob saw Esau coming with his army of men. Jacob bowed low seven times, and the Word says, "Esau ran to meet him and embraced him affectionately and kissed him; and both of them were in tears!" (Gen. 33:4, TLB).

Life can deal some unfair blows to all of us. But when God's sovereign power moves through repentance and forgiveness, a miracle takes place. We see this in the lives of Jacob and Esau. Not only had God done a mighty work in Jacob's life, but Esau also had changed. Esau was able to forgive his brother for stealing his birthright and blessing. Time has a way of healing the hearts of people so restoration can be possible. Esau and Jacob were able to put aside their hurts and wounds and let God's healing power pour over their lives and the lives of their families.

Much like Jacob's old nature had changed, when we got saved, we left our old ways of doing things behind. When we pour out our old nature and yield it to Jesus as Lord of our lives, then, and only then, can God give us a new name. A new identity will emerge from each one of us.

Each time someone is given a new name, a change takes place in his or her character. We see this in the life of Jacob when he immediately responded to his brother in humility, honor and love. Esau could only respond to his brother with a tearful embrace.

What about you? Do you recognize the changes that have taken place in your character because you've exchanged your old life for a new life? Do you realize how many people you have affected differently because Jesus is Lord of your life?

I know when Christ's blood was poured out over my sin and the shame of my past, my life immediately began to affect my family, especially my dad. Light and darkness do not mix. Therefore, the light I was reflecting to my dad penetrated any form of darkness in his life.

I remember coming home from a youth retreat one time. I was all fired up and singing some song about being "all wrapped up and tied up and tangled up in Jesus." This went on for about ten minutes because I was so excited about what God had done in my life, and I thought, *Everyone will want to have what I have.* Well, my dad couldn't stand all this light shining so brightly in his house. So he asked rudely, "Laurie, would you just be quiet for a while?" I felt stunned and wounded. My newfound faith in Jesus was not going to be embraced quite so quickly in my home. My dad couldn't handle all the joy in my life because the life he was living was producing only death.

I was too young (fifteen at the time) to realize the effects of this power that was poured out over my life because of what Jesus did on the cross for me. This power began to shake my dad's world to the core. Dad had to sit by and watch his daughter's shame be replaced with God's amazing glory while he was still experiencing tremendous shame in his own life. Dad couldn't help but notice all the changes that were taking place in my life. This was happening only because God began to reveal Himself in new ways to me. Then I was able to fulfill the destiny God had given me through my testimony of what He had done for me.

Little did I know that by accepting Jesus into my heart, not only would I change the course of my destiny, but my family's destiny would be changed, too. There is power in a transformed life.

Are you ready to make a name change and see how God uses your transformed life? Are you persistent enough to press through your past as Jacob did and wrestle all night for a new name? Are you willing to climb any mountain in your life so you can get to the top, where the blessings of the Lord are waiting for you? As you read this next story, try to allow the Holy Spirit to speak to you and encourage you to make a name exchange.

When I train for marathons, I run many miles to

improve my endurance and climb many hills for strength training. One day, my friend Linda was riding her bike with me while I was running a ten- to fifteen-mile endurance run. On our jaunt, we prayed together for our church's needs, and soon we began to climb a hill.

As we approached the hill, Linda took off on her bike, and I climbed the hill step by step. We reached the top of the hill at different times, both out of breath, yet both exhilarated that we had made it to the top. Going down was much easier. We had the fresh morning air on our faces and the wind cooling us down. The view of the valley was spectacular. We reached the bottom, turned around and ran back up the hill. This takes discipline, endurance and commitment.

After we conquered the hill the second time, Linda shared her heart with me. When we are walking through hurt and pain, it's like climbing a hill or wrestling all night for a new name. Although we all have experienced shame differently because of our various life experiences, all of us want to leave our past behind us. But most of the time, our shame will try to keep us from rising above it.

We will all reach the top of our mountains at different times because some shame issues can take longer to heal than others. Don't be discouraged if you feel stuck in your pain for a while. Persevering through our pain is part of the process of dealing with shame. On some days, we may even feel we will never make it to the top of our mountain because our pain and shame can keep us from even trying to run our daily race.

Just as with Jacob, there is a cost involved when our past is full of lies, schemes and tricks. Just as when we run ten miles and climb a hill in the middle of the run, there is a price to pay in training so we can finish the race for which we have been preparing.

When we deal with shame issues in our lives, sometimes we may even feel like giving up, turning around and going back to the comfort of our past. Many times, I have thought, *It's just too hard to climb to the top and rise above my hurt and pain.*

But what we don't realize is that our struggle to press through our situations to reach the top and conquer our pain and shame results in the power of God reaching into our lives, restoring us and giving us a new identity. Our focus must be on Jesus and how He pressed right through His own pain and persevered long enough to be able to die on the cross for our sin and shame. If Jesus was able to wrestle through His night of ultimate pain, we, too, can press through our pain and allow the power of the cross to conquer our shame.

In Luke 22:42, Jesus responded, "Father, if You are willing, remove this cup from Me; yet not My will, but [always] Yours be done" (AMP). Jesus was experiencing the ultimate cost of knowing He would pay the price for our sins and that He also would be separated from His Father. Jesus wasn't afraid to tell His Father how He was genuinely feeling, but He was also willing to do His Father's will.

Our response to our shame and pain should be the same: "Father, if You are willing, remove this cup from me; yet not my will, but Yours be done." We have to be willing to push through our pain to see the cross of Jesus defeat our shame.

If we do this, eternal rewards will be waiting for us at the top of each of our mountains. They are within our reach. But so many times, we give up too easily and turn around, only to have to start at the beginning and climb those mountains in our lives all over again.

What we need to do is stay on course and climb those mountains that God has asked us to climb. He will always be there with us. There is no reason to fear. Through every pain and disappointment, He will help us reach the top.

Recently, I've discovered one of the reasons that I don't like conflict is the pain strife caused me as a child. When conflict arises in my relationships, I just want to avoid the pain and back down and weep. I surrender quickly because this is how I have always dealt with conflict. We all have certain coping mechanisms that we like to revert to.

Jesus is showing me that I can no longer deal with conflict in this manner. It's time for me to grow up, let Jesus heal me and move on. When I keep my eyes on Jesus and not on my emotions, my past can no longer keep me captive. I am set free, and I feel like I can breathe again.

God has so much in store for each of us that He wants us to surrender all our pain and shame to Him. If we only give Him some of our past, the rest is still hidden deep within our hearts, keeping us from receiving the fullness of life that God has for us.

This is one of the greatest deceptions of the enemy, who tells us, "It's too painful to reveal your pain and shame. What will others think of you? Your past is too bad and full of sin. No one could love or even forgive you now." The enemy will try to use this to keep us from releasing our past. That is because he knows if we exchange our past, the power of God's glory will begin to stream through our lives, and others will be affected tremendously by it. We all need to know the incredible impact our freedom might have on someone.

We all have something in our past that we are not proud of. We have all done many things that we would like to change, but we cannot go back and change the past.

The only One who can do anything about our past is Jesus. His healing power can restore double anything that our past has taken from us. The only way we can leave our past behind and be free from it is because of the blood of Jesus that was shed on the cross for us. We have been forgiven, and now we have the keys to move forward and leave our past behind us.

We may never forget the past, but we can be free from it when we realize all our sins, even the ones from the past, can be forgiven. When we exchange our guilt and shame, God will replace it with many new things. Our anger can be exchanged for His gentleness and peace. Our fear will be replaced with His love and courage. Our shame will be traded for His glory.

Our character has been strengthened because we have walked through these difficult places and we have made many exchanges. As we press forward, we begin to run the race God has called us to run. (See Philippians 4:13–14.) Let us run toward the prize that God has called us to share. He wants us to be clothed in His robe of righteousness.

> He will give:
>> Beauty for ashes;
>> Joy instead of mourning;
>
> Praise instead of heaviness.
>
> —ISAIAH 61:3, TLB

Everything God has to offer us is far better than anything this world can give us.

Our ultimate reward is eternity with the King of kings. Therefore, we must change our way of thinking. We must re-evaluate what we allow our minds to dwell on. Are you allowing your thoughts to wander back to the things of the past, or are you focusing on the things that God has for you? A simple way to answer that is to observe your thoughts for a day.

The Word will help you redirect your thoughts. It says:

> Fix your thoughts on what is true and good and right. Think about things that are pure and lovely, and dwell on the fine, good things in others. Think about all you can praise God for and be glad about.
> —PHILIPPIANS 4:8, TLB

As we press forward, we must exchange our thoughts of worthlessness and shame for God's thoughts. If we dwell on the truth, then the truth will set us free.

Just as focusing on God can bring glory to those around us, continuing to dwell on our past affects others as well.

If I spent my days dwelling on the things in my family's past, my children and my husband would be affected by it. For example, if I had never forgiven my parents, I would still be bitter and walking in unforgiveness. This would greatly affect how I love other people, especially my husband and children. But because I have traded the shame of my family's past for Christ's freedom, I am now free to genuinely love my husband and children. I am free; therefore, my mind is set free to dwell on the good things of God, and I've watched how my character has changed.[1]

After we have worked on training our thoughts, we

need to allow God to show us how He wants to use us to be a world-changer for Him. You may be thinking, *How can I be a world-changer?* Begin by praying. Recognize the immediate need for prayer for this world. Then repent for your sin of prayerlessness.

Someone somewhere prayed you into the Kingdom. It could have been a great-grandmother, a family member or a friend. We may never know who paid the price in prayer for us. Yet all of us need to understand the call of God on our own lives and begin to pray without ceasing.

> I will not cease to pray for her or to cry out to God on her behalf until she shines forth in His righteousness and is glorious in His salvation.
>
> —ISAIAH 62:1, TLB

I know the Lord has called me to pray. I believe that praying without ceasing is like training for a marathon. When training, you build up your miles slowly so you can get into shape. You can begin praying just by coming to God and asking Him to forgive you for anything that could block your relationship with Him. Then, after you have established a clean heart, you can ask God to show you how to pray or whom to pray for. Just wait a few minutes and see if God will bring to your mind what He wants you to do. I'm sure He will impress upon you someone who needs prayer or maybe even a visit from you. This will begin to build up your prayer life.

With running, after you have built up miles, you are ready to add hills, speed training and endurance miles. These efforts will increase your stamina and help build up other muscles that need strengthening. Similarly, you then become ready to strengthen your prayer life. In this process, God may begin to ask you to rise up early to pray. This requires self-discipline to deny your flesh and get out of bed in the morning. God may even ask you to fast certain mealtimes or to set aside a specific time to seek His face and pray. He may even ask you to begin to pray corporately with other people from your church.

When you run many miles, you have to learn to refuel your body with the right foods and liquids. This will help you perform better, and your body will have a quicker recovery time after each workout. In prayer, you need recovery time also, especially when you are praying for others. When we pray intently for others, we can begin to carry their burdens. This can weigh us down. We must always give this burden over to the Lord. It is His to carry because He was the One who paid the greatest price for it. My prayer recovery time may start with refueling with the bread of life (the Bible), and end with worship, thanking my Lord and Savior for all He has done.

Now you are more than ready to run your marathon because you have been faithful and trained hard. It's the same with prayer. After all the asking, seeking and knocking, God will open up the windows of heaven and rain down answers to your requests. If you don't pray, the opposite will happen: Your requests will go unanswered. As with running, if you don't get your miles in, you will never finish the race. We must pray and intercede and give God no rest until the cries of our hearts have been heard.

In 1998, I felt that God wanted me to run a marathon for my church so that He could answer the last prophetic word that was spoken over my church when it began some twenty-five years ago. The prophecy said that people would be lined up outside waiting to get into

Christ's Center Church. I believe that is God's heart for every church in every nation. Another word that was given was: "I don't want just another body formed there. I want self-desires and self-wills dead. My desires are love for men's souls, peace for their lives, joy for their spirit. This will come by submission by you and wisdom from Me only. If you will give yourself totally, you will be usable by Me. I will build My church, not you." This is why I feel called to pray for my church.

If we are to die to ourselves, it will begin with prayer. If we have a heart for the lost, it will come by being on our knees. Peace will come, and joy will follow. We must yield our own plans and desires to God's way of doing things. When we give ourselves totally to God and not withhold one thing from the Lord, we will become usable vessels. God can then build His church because our flesh is out of the way.

Since our church split more than ten years ago, many of us have prayed for God to take off the shame and dishonor that has cloaked our church and replace it with His glory. He has done so in a remarkable way.

One way he has done this is by the incredible relationships we have with our friends in the alliance. God has blessed us far beyond our imagination.

If you come into our church, you will see a gym ceiling lined with flags. Many of us from Christ's Center have gone to dozens of nations and have been blessed with deep, enduring friendships with people all over the world because God has removed our shame and given us a new name.

We have prayed for God to give us a new reputation in our city, one that God "delights in," and we are seeing Him do just that. I believe God has done this by giving us a new in-house pastor in David and Judy Kauffman. Our founding pastor, Jon Bowers, and his wife, Lynna Gay, are busy flying all over the world to keep in touch with all our alliance friends. Dave and Judy are now in charge of the surrounding areas in our city.

I believe every church in every city needs to shine forth like a beacon, and people will be blinded by all the glory they see. People will be drawn to the light because the world is becoming so dark. It all starts with you and me; we are called to be those intercessors on the walls who will cry to God all day and all night for the fulfillment of His promises.

Isaiah 62:6–7 tells us to "take no rest, all you who pray, and give God no rest until He establishes Jerusalem and makes her respected and admired throughout the earth" (TLB). I want to see people lined up at my church waiting to come in. I want to see Christ's Center be that light shining brightly for all the world to see.

God's glory is the drawing force that will cause people to see that we are different. When people are attracted to you, it is because of the glory of the Lord shining in your life. It is not because you are so good looking or that you do something special. It is all because of what God has done in your life and the glory of the Lord that rests on your face.

So start your day with prayer, and keep on praying throughout the day. Pray in the car. Pray while you do dishes. Pray in the supermarket checkout line. Pray at the hardware store. Pray at work. Pray, pray, pray!!! End each day with prayer, and don't forget to thank the One who has given you so much.

The glory of the Lord rested on me the moment I

received Christ. It was the greatest moment in my life. When I lifted my hand, I felt God change me. Even my appearance changed. I glowed, and I was filled with peace and joy. I couldn't contain my unspeakable joy. I wanted everyone to know that something special had happened in my life. I was forever changed.

Think back on the time you got saved. Can you remember where you were in your life? Do you remember how you felt the minute you received Jesus as Lord of your life?

When my life changed, people took notice. Some didn't understand it, but others were curious and wanted to know what was different about me. God was holding me "aloft in his hands for all to see—a splendid crown for the King of kings" (Isaiah 62:3, TLB).

I remember going back to school the summer after I was saved. My friends noticed I was different. They could tell just by the look on my face. One of my best friends asked me what had happened to me, and so I shared my story with her in choir class. God's glory fell between two best friends, and she got saved right there in class.

God had given me a new name, and now He had given my friend a new name also. The Lord was delighting in both of us, and He was claiming us as His own. It felt incredible to belong to the Lord. I had a family now, and I was adopted into the broader family of the King of all kings.

Now when I read scripture such as Romans 8:15–17, I feel it was written just for me. "And so we should not be like cringing, fearful slaves, but we should behave like God's very own children, adopted into the bosom of His family, and calling to him, 'Father, Father.' For His Holy Spirit speaks to us deep in our hearts, and tells us that we really are God's children. And since we are His children, we will share His treasures—for all God gives to His Son Jesus is now ours too. But if we are to share His glory, we must also share His suffering" (TLB).

Jesus came to die for us, so we can share in His glory and His treasures. What God gave to His Son He freely gives to each of us, and He holds nothing back from us. It is ours to receive. We get to live eternally in heaven, free from pain and suffering. We have full rights as His children. When we get to heaven, we will receive new bodies and never be sick again. We will live forever. What a God we serve!

I am willing to share God's glory with those around me. Are you? I am willing to be a light. Are you? I am willing to reflect His image wherever I go. Are you? Let's be world-changers! Let's begin and end with prayer.

Prayer moves the hand and the heart of God. God has a call upon your life. God has a ministry that He wants to give you: loving people. We all have a need to be loved and to give that love away.

When God changed our hearts, He filled them with His unconditional love. We need to take that love and reach the unreachable, touch the untouchable. We need to love the unlovely.

> The Spirit of the Lord God is upon me, because the Lord has anointed me to bring good news to the suffering and afflicted. He has sent me to comfort the broken-hearted, to announce liberty to captives and to open the eyes of the blind.
>
> —ISAIAH 61:1, TLB

Each of us has the Spirit of the Lord upon our lives.

Each of us has an anointing to make a difference in the world around us.

> Arise, my people! Let your light shine for all the nations to see! For the glory of the Lord is streaming from you. Darkness as black as night shall cover all the peoples of the earth, but the glory of the Lord will shine from you. All nations will come to your light; mighty kings will come to see the glory of the Lord upon you"
>
> —Isaiah 60:1–3, TLB

We need to be attentive to see whose life we could touch on any given day. The world is aching and sending us all kinds of clues that it is dying.

Pray for God to give you a vision for your world around you—your family, your neighborhood, your cities—and then let's take this nation by storm. God takes broken people like you and me and uses us to bring good news to the suffering and afflicted people in this world.

Let God use your brokenness to touch people's lives for His Glory. God's glory wants to stream from you to shine bright in this dark world. We are the light for all the world to see. People will be attracted to us, and we will be able to offer them what Jesus gave us: His unfailing love. Ask God to give you His heart for this world and for the lives of the people around you. We need to get out of the church and into this world for the cause of Christ. Our mission field is the ground beneath our feet.

How do we love people the way they need to be loved? How do we turn the other cheek when someone slaps us in the face? The following story shows how I did this growing up.

When you are living for Jesus in an unsaved home, the

task of loving others and turning the other cheek even when they don't love you back is a difficult one. I was faced with this task when I was young.

After my parents' divorce, I didn't want anything to do with my mom. She had left me, and for that shame, I felt like punishing her and never speaking to her again. A year had gone by between then and the time I asked Jesus into my heart. I received Jesus before either of my parents did. One of the first things Jesus asked me to do was to love my parents and to honor them at all costs. Both of them were hurting, broken people at the time, so you can only imagine the depths I went to trying to love my parents with my newfound love in Jesus. Jesus asked me to start spending time with my mom again. This was going to be difficult for me because I had hardly spoken to her in a year. But it was going to be even more difficult for my dad because he would have to face sharing me with his ex-wife.

I remember the first Saturday morning that I was going to spend time with her. I had been my dad's little girl, and he didn't want to share me with anyone. But I was a young girl wanting so much to honor God by honoring and loving my parents. When I told my dad I was going to spend the day with Mom, you would have thought a bomb had exploded in the house. Dad lost control and started yelling at me, saying, "How could you go and spend time with this woman after all she has done to us?" Time seemed to stand still, and I remember feeling my dad's painful words seep deeply into my spirit. This went on for about thirty minutes. I sat in a chair, weeping uncontrollably. My mind raced, and I felt varying emotions. I thought, *Why am I the one to blame? I didn't cause this divorce. I just wanted to do the right thing.* I felt so hopeless, all I could do was sit there and bear the burden of my dad's shame.

When my mom came, I was in tears and looked a mess. *What had I done so wrong to cause my dad to react so strongly?* I felt torn by two worlds. Jesus told me to love even when I was not getting the same love back.

> Listen, all of you. Love your enemies. Do good to those who hate you. Pray for the happiness of those who curse you; implore God's blessing on those who hurt you. If someone slaps you on one cheek, let him slap the other too! If someone demands your coat, give him your shirt besides. Give what you have to anyone who asks you for it; and when things are taken away from you, don't worry about getting them back. Treat others as you want them to treat you.
> —Luke 6:27–31, TLB

Here I was trying to love my mom after not speaking to her for an entire year. And in spite of this, I still felt as if I were betraying my dad by leaving him at home. Staying at home with Dad might have made him happy, but it wouldn't have done anything to mend my broken relationship with Mom.

Shame at that moment was making me feel like no matter what I did, it would never be right or good enough. Remember, shame comes from Satan, not from God. He was using it in my life to discourage and destroy me. He was also using the person closest to me to impute that shame. But Satan didn't win; God did. I have victory in my life because Jesus redeemed back to me that which was stolen from me. When you love a person unconditionally, it frees you and the other people involved from the shame that can come from the pain of your past.

If I had never started to love my mom again, who knows where our relationship would be today. Or worse yet, where would my relationship be with my own daughter? Sometimes we have to pay the price to be free so our own children will be free. I would pay any price to have a relationship with my children. So, if I had to turn the other cheek and feel the pain of shame and the dishonor of divorce, I would do it all over again.

Let God show you where you are broken. Whom have you shut out of your life? Stop right now and ask the Holy Spirit to show you. Now that you've taken the time to discover whom it is that you need to forgive, please pray the following prayer of forgiveness with me. It will set you and other people free.

> *Dear Jesus, please forgive me for holding others at arm's length. Please forgive me for taking up an offense and not forgiving those who have hurt me so much. I choose this day to forgive the individuals who have caused me so much pain. I turn this deep wound over to You, and I surrender it forever. Please replace this hurt and pain with Your love and peace. Thank You, Lord. Amen.*

If we stand in the gap and love even when genuine love isn't returned to us, it will make a difference in our lives, our children's lives and the lives of the people we are trying to love.

I am so glad I loved my dad even in his darkest hours. My mom and I are seeing God heal and restore our relationship. Now we are closer than we have ever been. She is a valuable person in my life who prays for me constantly.

All this didn't happen by chance. God's genuine love

touches hearts and changes lives. That's what happened to me, and that is what has happened to both of my parents. God used the shame and dishonor of divorce to bring each of us to a place of brokenness so that we could receive Jesus as Lord of our lives. I know it wasn't God's highest for my family, but He used it to bring salvation to us. For this reason, any pain or shame that I have suffered has been worth it. Any time that I have had to turn a cheek and give love in return, I would not change for a second.

Jesus has changed my heart and filled it with His love. He has taken the shame and dishonor off my life and replaced it with His amazing glory. He has given me a new name, and it is one in which He delights. I have a personal joke with the Lord. He has taken "Laurie" and replaced it with His "Glory." Now I no longer think of myself as the Laurie of the past. I think of myself as the "Glory" of the Lord, with a bright future filled with hope ahead of me.

I could write for days about all the incredible blessings God has placed in my life. It is overwhelming. Of course, the obvious ones are my wonderful husband and children. They are my greatest source of joy and encouragement. When I watch us all growing up together, my heart is so full of God's redeeming love upon my life.

Jesus wants to do the same for everyone. It is within reach. Keep climbing those hills and mountains in your life. Keep running the race and focus on Jesus. If you do this, you will have little reason to dwell on the shame and dishonor of your past.

We have all heard the saying, "Shame on you." I am declaring to you today, "Shame off you, and God's glory on you."

God wants this. He wants to give each of us a new identity in Christ. God wants to redeem to you that which was lost and give you a double portion of His prosperity and great joy. (See Isaiah 61:8.)

The blood of Jesus cleanses shame and removes the effects of shame off our lives. As the shame leaves, the glory of the Lord will fall upon our lives. Everywhere we go, we will reflect Jesus to the lost of this broken, dying world. As God anoints you with His love, His Grace and His Glory, you will be a light, beaming for all the world to see. You will radiate the glory of the Lord. It is the key to the harvest of the lost people in this world. As you focus on lighting up the darkness in the world around you, think about the following questions, and let God use you as He desires.

- Have you received a new identity from the Lord, and has He given you a new name for yourself? Ask God to give you a new name. It might be as funny as mine, from Laurie to Glory.

- What "mountain" in your life has God asked you to climb? What is your mountain made of? Is it fear, anger, unforgiveness? What are you learning from it?

- God has called you to change your world. What has God asked you to do so this might happen?

- Think of an occasion where you had to turn the other cheek. What were the results of your doing this?

God gave me this song in 1998. It's called "World-Changers." Please read the words, and let them touch your life.

I'll be Your world-changer. You are my Creator. So now let's enter in, and let the healing begin. And let the healing begin.

You've touched my heart. And You've changed my life. You've clothed me with righteousness. You've set this captive free, giving liberty. Now I stand in faith, because of Your amazing grace.

I'll be Your world-changer. You are my Creator. So now let's enter in, and let the healing begin. And let the healing begin.

You bore my sin and pain. Covering my guilt and shame. Now You've crowned me with a brand-new name. I lift my voice in praise. To only You I raise. This song I sing, my life I bring to You.

I'll be Your world-changer. You are my Creator. So now let's enter in, and let the healing begin. And let the healing begin.

[1] Other suggested reading on the subject of our thoughts: Joyce Meyer's *The Battlefield of the Mind*, on how to change your thought life, and Francis Frangipane's *The Three Battlegrounds*, which will challenge your thoughts.

NINE

Touching Hearts, Changing Lives

No one has felt greater love for us than our heavenly Father and His Son Jesus. God's genuine love touches our hearts and changes our lives forever when we accept Jesus as Lord of our lives. Because of God's deep, enduring love, we hold in our hearts a much greater love than this world has to offer us.

And now is the time for us to use it. Besides reflecting Jesus and changing the lives of the lost in this world, there are unlimited practical ways we can touch people's hearts on a smaller scale every day. Then we can watch Jesus change their lives.

In John 15:12–13, Jesus commanded us to love one another just as He loved us. "No one has greater love [no one has shown stronger affection] than to lay down [give up] his own life for his friends" (AMP). Jesus gave up His own life for us, and now He is asking us to do the same for one another.

Are we really capable of giving up our lives for a friend? In our daily lives, how often do we rise in the morning and ask God what is on His heart for the day? Most of us just go through the motions of our day. Our mornings must look very repetitive to God.

My mornings look like this: I wake up, start making lunches, then wake the children up and get them moving. I start breakfast and then try to keep everyone going so we'll make it to school and work on time. I may pick up some coffee on the drive just to get my engine started.

Your mornings may be more relaxed. You may wake up slowly, read the paper, have some coffee and then decide what you're going to do next.

On the other hand, some people have their days fully planned weeks in advance, and nothing could interrupt their schedule unless it was a family emergency or pre-planned vacation.

Most of us do not have the luxury of having our days set in stone. It seems my days are easily interrupted by something or someone needing my attention. And often-times, it is the most important people in my life that I can easily overlook.

I can be up two hours in the mornings before I realize I could have touched a life already. Most of us are so busy in the mornings getting our families ready that we can miss opportunities to change lives. Many times, we seem to forget what an impact we are having on the lives of the people we love most. Unfortunately, it can be our family members whom we take for granted.

For instance, I may miss giving a needed hug or an extra word of encouragement to brighten someone's day. In my life, I must constantly be sensitive to what the Holy Spirit prompts me to do each morning. If I am alert to the needs of those in my family, I can be a vessel of love to help jump-start their day.

For example, one morning, I made my husband's lunch, and I tried to put all the things he likes in it. Then I wrote him a short note of encouragement about how thankful I am for him because he works so hard to provide for our family. This might not seem like a big thing to do, but I know it blessed my husband just because I thought of him.

Another example in my family is I know my oldest child needs more encouragement to get him motivated in the mornings than my other children require. He likes to wake up slowly, and I know rushing him or nagging him won't help. While my youngest two are up early, ready to start their day.

I usually go up to my oldest son's room, open his blinds, and then gently shake him until he's awake. Sometimes he likes me to visit with him in the morning. I could just bust into his room and yell, "Get up," but I know the effects of that rude awakening would dampen his spirit. I also know that I would miss out on our morning visits if I woke him up in a hurry.

Another thing our family did was surprise our youngest son with his heart's desire for his tenth birthday. He had wanted a puppy for so long, and we decided he was old enough to care for one. You should have seen the glee in his eyes as we stopped to pick up his puppy. He was surprised, and his entire body wiggled with joy.

Later, we had so much fun just watching him run and play in the yard with his new puppy, which he named Samson. Nothing could have brought us more joy that day than knowing we had found the key to touch our son's heart. As parents, we had been listening for months as Adam declared to us what his heart's desires were. All we did was listen and then be part of fulfilling that joy. He thanked us a million times with lots of hugs and kisses. Samson will be a great source of happiness for our son. He will long remember his tenth birthday and probably will tell stories about it for years to come.

All of us should ask God to give us ideas to bless the hearts of those we love. In my family, my husband and each child require something different because each of them has different characteristics and needs.

For instance, my sweet daughter has totally different needs than her brothers. She just loves to be with me no matter what we're doing. If I tried to love her the way I love her brothers, it wouldn't touch her life in the same way that it touches theirs.

Try this for a week, at home or at work, and see how it positively affects the lives of people around you: Ask God to show you on any given day who might need a word of encouragement. I promise, God will direct you. All you need to do is ask Him what to do, then follow through.

Many times, God must laugh at us and wonder why everyone is in such a hurry every day. Running to and fro, we must look like a bunch of bees buzzing around. Have you ever been on the main streets of New York City during the morning hours? There is a sea of people rushing from one place to another. When I was there, my first instinct was to try to stop someone and ask, "Why all the hurrying?," but I didn't have the courage. All the people seemed intent on fulfilling their days with whatever task was at hand. I wondered, *Does anyone ever stop to smell the flowers or do a kind act for someone? Does anyone ever take a stroll in Central Park or pause by the harbor just to relax and enjoy life?*

I am from a small, slow-moving, farming community. There always seemed to be enough time in a day to smell the flowers or enjoy watching a child play. But I think no matter where we live or what job we have, we must find time to enjoy our lives to the fullest—and that includes blessing others' hearts the way God blesses ours.

God loves us abundantly and has so much to give us that He is always waiting with outstretched arms for us. God knows what will bless our hearts, and He desires to give us the things in our lives that we take delight in. He always has time for us. He is continually looking for ways to encourage and bless us. He longs for us to take the time to be with Him. Just like we knew what would bless our son's heart on his tenth birthday, God knows what will bless our hearts. All we need to do is abide in His love and let Him help us through each day.

The word *abide* in the Greek means "to remain, to stay." "Abiding in the vine" means abiding in God's Word and keeping Jesus' commands. Every believer who remains in Jesus, who is careful to learn from God's Word and to obey His commands, will be fruitful. It is God's design that believers should live in union with His Son and become fruitful, that is, express the effect of their union with Jesus in their daily lives. This is what glorifies the Father—a changed heart and a changed life."

I believe to be able to abide, we must learn to begin and end our days in rest, because if we are abiding or dwelling in the Father, the Son and the Holy Spirit, our day will begin and end with rest.

When we abide in our relationship with Jesus, it causes us to be more open to His encouragement to bless someone else. If we learn how to rest in Jesus, peace, joy, hope, love and many other gifts of the Spirit will begin to blossom in our lives. He shows us how to rest.

> Dwell in Me, and I will dwell in you. [Live in Me, and I will live in you.] Just as no branch can bear fruit of itself without abiding in (being vitally united to) the vine, neither can you bear fruit unless you abide in Me. I am the Vine; you are the branches. Whoever lives in Me and I in him bears much (abundant) fruit. However, apart from Me [cut off from vital union with Me] you can do nothing"
>
> —JOHN 15:4–5, AMP

According to this scripture, if we live in Jesus, He promises to live in us. If we live our lives in vital union with Him, we will bear fruit in our daily lives. But if we don't take the time to be in a relationship with Jesus, we cannot bear any fruit, and we can do nothing of value that could touch hearts or change lives.

A great illustration of this might be a nursing infant who depends on her mother's "fruit" for nourishment and survival. Even when a baby is bottle-fed, she depends on her mother for comfort and love. When you have quiet time, reflect on Isaiah 66:11. Hear what God may speak into your heart. Ask Him how you could touch a life today. I promise, it will be a day that will bear much fruit.

I believe that if we dwell completely in Jesus, we will

be satisfied, and we will be delighted with more abundance and glory than we can handle. Furthermore, if we immerse ourselves in Jesus, He will show us what to do in our daily lives that could touch the hearts of others.

How do you immerse yourself in Jesus? It's not hard, but your busy life will try to complicate your efforts. Personally, I try to find quality time every day to be in a relationship with Jesus. Sometimes these are small segments of time filled with reading my Bible or worshiping on my piano. Other times, I just sit outside on the patio and relax and enjoy His presence by viewing His creation. I love the fresh smell of a summer breeze. I enjoy the fragrance of the flowers in bloom. I relax, close my eyes and bask in the warm morning sun. Sometimes these are the times when I am my best because I am at rest. These are the times I can hear from God because my mind is still and completely focused on Him.

Recently, I experienced the joy of having my heart touched. I was speaking at a chapel service, and I was glad I took time to seek the Lord that morning. I had been overseeing a group of young adults for two years, and I never dreamed my investment of abiding in Jesus and asking Him what He wanted for each chapel service could pay off so greatly.

With a teacher's direction and encouragement, these young men and women wrote letters of inspiration and gave them to me at our last chapel service of the school year. There was no greater gift anyone could have given me that day that would have blessed my heart more. One of the notes said it all. A young man wrote, "Dear Laurie, You gave me the best thing in the world by sharing the Word of God, and I want to give you this gift." I was overcome with emotion. He had told his mother that God had asked him to buy me a special tea cup as a gift of appreciation. He paid for this gift with his own money. I told him his gift would sit in a place of honor in my house where I could see it every day to remind me of God's love and encouragement to me. Now when I'm feeling low, I know I can read these cards and letters and let them touch my heart over and over again.

Sometimes we feel that what we do isn't valuable or isn't really sinking in to someone's life. Then God uses unexpected vessels to encourage us and overwhelm us with His love. Here, these young adults took the time to write something meaningful to bless someone else. I think they are the ones who grasped the concept of dwelling in Jesus. They heard what He wanted them to do; this touched my heart and changed my life forever. I will never be the same again because of the powerful words that flowed from their hearts.

And here I had chosen to immerse myself in Jesus. I knew that if I didn't spend time with Jesus praying for these students and crying out for God's heart for them, they would somehow pick up on it. I have learned that children will be the first to know if you are not abiding in the vine. They can sense genuine love and acceptance, and when someone is faking it. I knew that if I tried to do something in my own strength, I would fail miserably, and the children would be influenced by my lack of abiding in Jesus.

Often we try to do things in our own strength and within our own time frame. We don't invite Jesus along for the day because we are too busy and He would just get in the way and slow us down. These are the days we need to abide in the Lord the most. These are the days we should be on our knees for an hour before we begin our day.

I know this because I have done it both ways. I have started my day without Jesus and just about ran over everyone in my path. I can be one of those highly motivated people who like to accomplish a lot in any given day.

For instance, my husband and I like to get all the yard work done in one day. We have a fairly big yard, so it takes our entire family to accomplish this. Our children, who are old enough to help, don't see why we have to work so hard. They don't enjoy yard work, especially if we're putting on bark dust for ground cover. It has become a family joke that when our neighbor puts on her ground cover, I begin to tease my children that it is almost time for us to do ours. The only problem is that they tease me back because my neighbor does her yard work by herself, and they think I should, too.

As we begin our annual day of yard work, attitudes can easily fly because our children get testy and tired, and we lack patience and words of encouragement. They can easily forget that in exchange for yard work, they get to go to summer camps. Like our children, even young adults get to learn to make exchanges.

Sometimes on these days, there is no fruit that can be picked from my life because I have an agenda, and I know what I want to get done. Other days, I wake up and begin to pray before my feet hit the ground, and I invite Jesus to have His way in my life. All the people I meet during the day are glad because, when I'm abiding in Jesus, I am at my best, and I can be capable of loving people, especially my family.

Those are the days I feel peace, joy and love, and my

life bears much fruit because I am living in Jesus and He is living in me.

The alternative to not living in the vine and abiding in our relationship with our Lord is death. We must receive our nourishment from the Lord, or our relationship with Jesus will fade and die.

> If a person does not dwell in Me, he is thrown out like a [broken-off] branch, and withers; such branches are gathered up and thrown into the fire, and they are burned. If you live in Me [abide vitally united to Me] and My words remain in you *and* continue to live in your hearts, ask whatever you will, and it shall be done for you. When you bear (produce) much fruit, My Father is honored *and* glorified, and you show *and* prove yourselves to be true followers of Mine.
>
> —John 15:6–8, AMP

Have you ever had a close friend walk away from Jesus because of sin? When someone is loving God and then something pops up to distract the person from Jesus, it breaks her fellowship not only with God, but also with others. No longer is this person attached to the vine. She has broken her relationship with God, and she is not bearing fruit. She no longer has peace or joy. She begins to develop an edge in her attitude, which pushes people away from her. If she continues in this state of sin and rebellion, she will no longer receive her nourishment from the Lord, and her relationship with Jesus will die. When this happens, the Father is no longer glorified, and her prayers will go unanswered.

Like my friend, Adam and Eve fell from the vine when they disobeyed God. When they were deceived, it was their choice to disobey God, and it immediately had a negative effect on their relationship with God. They were so covered by God's glory that they were naked and unashamed. As soon as they ate the forbidden fruit, their eyes were opened, and the glory of God left them. They realized for the first time that they were naked, which produced much shame in their lives. They tried to cover themselves, and they hid from God.

When people break fellowship with God, they go into hiding instead of abiding. They respond in anger, which is an emotion of shame. They begin to blame everyone else, which only imputes shame on others. Soon they stop coming to church. People who walk in sin experience so much shame that they shut out even those closest to them. The effects of sin and shame then run rampant in their lives and in their innocent children's lives. People don't realize the generational shame that will be passed on to their children if they don't repent of their sins.

The opposite is true when we do everything in our lives through God. The effects of shame can no longer penetrate our lives because we stay attached to the vine. Just as a vine won't bear as much fruit if it is not pruned, we won't yield as much fruit in our lives if our sin and shame isn't pruned.

Complete surrender of our sin and shame is the only way His Word will remain in our lives and continue to live in our hearts. Then when we pray, He will hear our prayers, and hearts and lives can be changed. The Father is honored and glorified when we bear much fruit for His kingdom. When we love our children and honor our mates, God is glorified. When we stop what we are doing to listen to others and make them feel important, God is honored. This is laying down our lives to allow Jesus to touch hearts through us and change lives forever because of His great love dwelling in us.

There are two very different approaches to abiding in the vine. Luke 10:40–42 tells about two sisters, Martha and Mary, who loved Jesus very much. We find Martha overly occupied, even distracted with serving. She becomes disgusted with her sister because Mary isn't helping enough. Martha asks Jesus to tell Mary to come help her. I like Jesus' response: "Martha, Martha, you are anxious and troubled about many things; There is need of only one or *but a few things*. Mary has chosen the good portion [that which is to her advantage], which shall not be taken away from her" (AMP).

Many of us let all the things we have to do in our day cloud God's primary purpose for our lives. There are a lot of Marthas in this world who serve and serve. There is nothing wrong with serving. If we didn't serve, nothing would get done.

But when serving keeps us from sitting at the feet of Jesus and listening to what is on His heart, we miss out in our love relationship with our Savior. At this point, we are so busy "doing" that sometimes we don't remember *why* we are doing these things in the first place. In this scripture, Jesus is telling us that many of us do a lot of good things but fill our days so full that we never get a chance to sit and listen to Him.

When we are devoted in our relationship with Jesus, we cannot wait for time alone with Him. Like Mary, we long to be close to Him and experience all He has for our lives. Mary simply wanted to be close to Jesus to worship Him. It was at His feet that she felt secure, yet humbled.

With Jesus, Mary could be herself and share her heart. She gave all of her attention and affection to Jesus, and she lost herself in this relationship. Sometimes she was ridiculed by her sister because of her choices, yet she placed her relationship with Jesus above everything else in her life.

Martha, on the other hand, chose to serve Jesus. She was strong, rational, able to take charge and speak her mind. She was busy working and became anxious. Martha had a plan and an agenda. She knew what needed to be done and how to get it done. She was in a hurry, and she was in charge.

Martha met temporal needs with the labor of her hands. With this service came honor from men and women as she served and provided for others and for Jesus. How many times have you left Jesus out of the picture because you were too busy doing good things? Have you plowed through others because you had something that needed to get finished?

I have hurt many people close to me without even knowing it. Sometimes we can get an attitude and say things such as, "Well, it has to be done, and I guess I am the only one to do it, so get out of my way and let me do it." We may not vocalize what we are thinking, but I'm sure many of us have thought this.

These are the times when we crush people with our attitudes and our actions. We will never know what God's primary purpose is if we act that way.

We need a balance between serving people and listening to Jesus. To be able to serve with a right heart and purpose, we must be listening to Jesus. If our hearts are in tune with God's heart, we can serve in any capacity and not get a wrong attitude.

Have you ever seen someone serve with an attitude? It makes you want to run from them. Serving with the right attitude causes people to want to serve along with you. Even in our mundane chores, we can touch hearts and change lives.

I once heard a friend share how much she hated to iron. One day as she started on the pile of clothes, she complained to God about her job. (Personally, I never would have thought to talk to God about ironing.) Then God asked her, "Whom are you serving while you are ironing?" Her response was, "You, Lord." To that, He said, "Then serve Me with your whole heart and quit complaining, even in the simple chores."

If you focus on Jesus, even the "little" jobs can be done with great joy. When you know you're serving Jesus by serving others, you'll know you are touching hearts and changing lives.

This is important for moms to keep in mind. Sometimes being a mom is the hardest job. All the laundry, cooking, cleaning and many other chores can go unnoticed by others. But Jesus sees our hearts. He knows what each of us has done behind the scenes. He sees what no one else sees; if we do everything as unto Him, then our everyday lives will be filled with blessings.

My pastor, Jon Bowers, is a good example. He often has a list of chores that his wife needs help with around the house. He likes to call these his "honey do's." I have never heard Pastor Jon complain about his list of "honey do's." He tries to do everything with joy, and his love for his wife is a constant example for us all.

My pastor has learned the art of abiding in Jesus, even

during mundane chores. He has learned the principle from God's Word: "If you lavish upon others, you yourself will be lavished upon. If you refresh others, you also will be refreshed."

> There are those who [generously] scatter abroad, and yet increase more; there are those who withhold more than is fitting *or* what is justly due, but it results only in want. The liberal person shall be enriched, and he who waters shall himself be watered.
>
> —Proverbs 11:24–25, AMP

You cannot be around Pastor Jon for long and not feel encouraged or refreshed. I remember the time I went to Pastors Jon and Lynna Gay's house to talk with them about my dad's disease. I felt so ashamed about my dad having AIDS that all I could do was cry. As they listened and allowed me to pour my heart out, I began to feel better; I knew they genuinely cared about me. Soon Pastor Jon was lightening my load by telling me one of his famous hysterical stories. I laughed for the next thirty minutes until my side ached. He refreshed me with laughter, and it helped me to bear an incomprehensible burden. Laughter truly can be the best medicine for a hurting heart. I experienced firsthand what being refreshed was all about in one of the darkest times of my life.

As my pastor lavished love on me through the gift of telling hilarious stories, I was able to exchange my shame for laughter and joy. Pastor Jon gave generously of his time and energy, and I'm sure the blessings of God came back to him.

Oftentimes, when we give, God supplies us with even more so we can give further. Can we possibly become richer by giving more? Our world says to hold on to what is ours because we've worked so hard to earn it. Isn't it awesome that God's ways are the opposite of the world's ways? This is true not only with our finances, but also with our time. When you give generously in ministry to others, God gives back to you overabundantly. You can never out-give God.

I have experienced God's generosity because of my commitment to pray for my church and my leaders. When you are lavishing blessings upon your church and the people in it, God enriches your life. Since I began praying for my church, I have been so blessed by the incredible presence of the Lord in my life. When I run, God touches me. When I worship Him in private or in public, I experience His love pouring over my life. I have never felt so blessed or encouraged in my life, all because God called me to pray for my church. and I obeyed.

I have prayed for shame and dishonor to fall away from my church, and I have seen God take the shame off my own life and lavish me with His glory. When the shame comes off your life, you are abiding in Jesus more, and you're able to give more. Therefore, there is more fruit coming from your life because shame no longer can detach you from the vine.

I have prayed for God to "enlarge the place of our tent." I've prayed that He do some remodeling in our church to better meet our needs, and now I am blessed because I got to enlarge my house. I have prayed for my church family members to give their whole hearts, souls and minds to the Lord, and I got to experience falling in love with Jesus all over again. My life has been full of blessings.

On the other hand, if you grumble or complain about things, whether in church or in your personal life, you will not be lavished upon. If you do not give out to others, your life will be void of the blessings of the Lord.

For example, when someone in ministry hurts or wounds us, our tendency is to shut them out of our lives. If we do this, we will soon begin to murmur and complain about the offense. Then we can become easily dissatisfied and look for other things to complain about. Before we know it, we have gotten ourselves so wound up in the offense that we are held tightly in its grip. If we take up an offense, the lavishing principle cannot work in our lives.

How do I know? I have done it. I have taken an offense and let it hold me captive. During these times, no fruit can be picked in my life. It seems that people avoid me because the fruit from my vine has spoiled. Now I am at a pruning stage in my life; I have no other choice but to repent for my sin of keeping an offense and to plead for God's forgiveness. Only then can I get back on track in my relationship with Jesus and with others.

Repentance and forgiveness are the keys to the blessings of the Lord on our lives. If we leave out one of these keys, we will not experience the glory of the Lord as we should, and we will not discover or fulfill His primary purpose for our lives.

I believe that, for God to do more in our lives and for us to experience an increase in our lives, we must be obedient to deal with shame. For us to walk in greater anointing, we must leave our past behind us.

God is not small. He is "eternally large." God thinks big, and He has great plans for you and me. We must not set our sights on small things. We must not wallow in our sin and shame. We need to dream a little and let God use our gifts to fulfill our primary purpose on earth. (See Ephesians 3:20.)

Get ready, Church. God is going to release all of us into doing things we never thought we could do. We must repent for our lack of faith. We must exchange our shame for His glory. We must take time to dream.

It's time to step across the line of mediocrity and start believing in the miracles that God wants to lavish upon our lives.

We are in the days of multiplication, not addition.

We are in the days of multiplication, not addition. God is ready to pour out His impartation to those who are ready to receive it. When we are released to pray for others, the release will come from heaven and the anointing will flow from our lives. Glory will shine forth from us for all the world to see.

> If My people, who are called by My name, shall humble themselves, pray, seek, crave, *and* require of necessity My face and turn from their wicked ways, then will I hear from heaven, forgive their sin, and heal their land.
> —2 CHRONICLES 7:14, AMP

We must be willing to humble ourselves to the place of being broken for our sins. We must repent and turn from our sins; only then will God hear from heaven and forgive us of our sins and heal our land. I don't know about you, but I am willing to pay the price in prayer and humble myself and repent so God can hear my prayers and begin to heal this land.

But we must repent for more than our own sins. There was a time in my life when I had to come to grips with the fact that my children could be affected if I didn't repent for the sins of my parents, grandparents or anyone from a previous generation. This was hard for me to do. I thought, *Why should I repent for their sins when I had nothing to do with them?* God had an astounding response: "Do you want generational sins to touch the lives of your children, or will you be willing to humble yourself and repent for the sins of your forefathers?" When God put it that way, I clearly understood. I knew that if I repented for the sins of my family, the enemy couldn't pass them on to my children or grandchildren. This would help my children live Godly lives, and bear fruit and get lavished on as a result.

However, if we don't stand in the gap and repent for our sins and the sins of our forefathers, they will show up in the lives of our children and their children as well.

> Keeping mercy *and* loving-kindness for thousands, forgiving iniquity and transgression and sin, but who will by no means clear the guilty, visiting the iniquity of the fathers upon the children and the children's children, to the third and fourth generation.
> —EXODUS 33:7, AMP

I didn't want divorce, homosexuality, unforgiveness, bitterness or any other sins to get passed on to my children or to their children. I would do anything to keep them from being affected by my sins or by those of my family lineage. I cried out in repentance and asked God for His unfailing love to forgive me and the sins of my forefathers. I felt complete peace, knowing that through the blood of Jesus, I could stand in the gap, and all the generational sins would be removed.

What a great exchange we can make, trading in the sins of our families and being covered with God's unfailing love and mercy. I no longer worry about generational sins affecting me or my children. I know my children may still struggle, but it will be their own doing. I am set free from fear, and so are my children and their children to come. What a miracle! It's the power of the cross and the Resurrection that sets captives free from sin.

Unfortunately, not everyone takes advantage of this awesome miracle today. We do see the effects of some parents' sins on the lives of their children. For example, we see children killing each other.

When children are abused, oftentimes they become abusers. Research validates this. I believe that, in many cases, this is why we see violence in schools. It is the enemy's goal to try to destroy our children, and he will use any avenue he can. He will use broken homes, violent music and many kinds of abuse to destroy our children's lives.

Abuse can come in many forms. It can be verbal (what people say or what they don't say), physical (from violent abuse to the lack of love and affection), or sexual (from a child being touched inappropriately to a child picking up a negative view of sexuality from their parents). If we give our children the wrong view of sexuality, it skews their view of their own sexuality.

For example, if you were raised in a home where extreme modesty was enforced, you may feel very self-conscious about your body. On the other hand, if you were raised in a home where modesty wasn't a big issue, you are probably more comfortable with your body.

I know in my life, I have had to renew my mind in the area of sexuality. I was never physically or sexually abused by my parents, but their choices of sexuality had a negative effect on my views. I have had to exchange their view of sexuality for God's view. Genuine intimacy can come only from understanding the love of God through His precious Son, Jesus. I am still making progress on this issue in my life. I am continuing to exchange my thoughts for God's thoughts.

> For My thoughts are not your thoughts, neither are your ways My ways, says the Lord. For as the heavens are higher than the earth, so are My ways higher than your ways and My thoughts than your thoughts.
>
> —ISAIAH 55:8–9, AMP

It is my constant prayer for all of us to allow God to give us His thoughts on sexuality. A negative view of sexuality stemming from childhood can keep you from wanting to be intimate. If you feel guilt or shame in this area for any reason, you may be extremely modest and choose to cover up or be in the dark during moments of intimacy.

This area of shame alone can be hard to overcome. It can be frustrating because you are unsure what deep shame still lies hidden in your life.

Whenever these feelings arise, you must give them over to the Lord and allow Him to remove this shame, layer by layer. Soon, this shame, like so many others we've exchanged, will come to the light because we have a clearer understanding and the maturity to deal with it.

Don't give up on yourself if you are fighting a similar battle in some area of your life. Don't let the enemy win. It is the enemy's scheme to try to trick us and hold us captive. He will do anything he can to keep us walking in shame. I combat this with complete surrender of every area of my life to my Lord and Savior. The enemy knows how powerful we will be when we get set free.

If you have never given up the shame of sexuality or any other shame, stop right now and turn it over to the Lord. He will heal your broken heart and bind up your wounds.

> Behold, I am doing a new thing! Now it springs forth; do you not perceive *and* know it *and* will you not give heed to it? I will even make a way in the wilderness and rivers in the desert.
>
> —ISAIAH 43:19, AMP

What God has done in our past is nothing compared to the miracles He wants to do for us now.

To see these miracles, we need to cry out to God for the forgiveness of our sins and the generational sins of our forefathers on behalf of our children and their children. We cannot ignore the widespread violence in the lives of our children any longer. We must pray for our future generations. All it takes is a repentant, humble heart. God will remove these sins as far as the east is from the west.

If you truly repent, it means your behavior will have to change. No longer will you be able to do things the way you used to. You must put away the things of the past and press forward into all that God has for you and your family.

Just as we must cry out to God for our children's sake,

we must do the same for our nation if we want to see our nation under God once again. When we stand in the gap and cry out with a repentant heart, God will hear from heaven, and then He can heal our land.

But we have to choose to make a stand and make a difference in our nation. God loves America; He has put His hand of blessing on it from the beginning. Now, as a nation, we have walked away from what our founding fathers believed. They understood the fear of the Lord, and they walked in it. Everything they did was in God and through God and with God. The Bible was the most important book from which to teach, even in public schools. Now the Bible cannot even appear on a teacher's desk. Now can you understand why there is so much violence in our schools? Our children have nowhere in the public school system to turn to for deep healing for their broken hearts.

So what will it be? Do you love this world more than you love God? Will you continue to tolerate the sin in your life, or will you repent and take a stand for living right? Are you breaking God's heart by living your life the way you do? How is your life affecting your children? Do you live your life to honor God, or do you live according to your own selfish ambitions?

We must first have a heart change, then a lifestyle change will follow. We cannot ride the fence of compromise any longer. We cannot be lukewarm in our relationship with Jesus. We need to be on fire and take a stand and turn from our sin. Our nation's children are depending on us. We must be the ones to make these generational exchanges for our children. If you are ready to stand in the gap for the children of this world, please pray with me:

Lord, we long to turn from our wicked ways as a nation. Please come and bring healing to our broken land. Lord, forgive us of our sins and selfishness. We repent and ask for Your forgiveness. We choose to stand in the gap for the generational sins of our nation so they will no longer affect our children. Please hear the cries of our hearts and restore to us a nation under God once again. Amen.

SOMETHING TO THINK ABOUT

- What causes us to bear fruit in our daily lives?

- What happens to us if we don't abide in the vine?

- What does Luke 10:40–42 speak to you personally? Describe Mary and Martha.

- What is God's principle about lavishing or refreshing? What is the world's view?

- Ask God to show you your primary purpose in the kingdom of God.

- Why must we pray, seek God's face, be humble and repent?

TEN

Wash Over Me

There is nothing like Your presence.
Oh, Lord, heal me with Your touch.
Your great and mighty power always lifts me up.
Fill me with compassion, overwhelm me by Your love.
Let Your grace and Your glory stream through this place.
Wash over me, by the power of Your Word.
As I live and as I breathe, oh, Lord, wash over me.
Wash over this nation, Father; Let Your kingdom come.
As we pray and as we seek Your face, oh, Lord, wash
over me.
And as the waters cover the sea, my Lord, wash over me.
                                            —LAURIE SMUCKER(1998)

I penned the words to this song on the way home from

my first trip to India. As I have privately worshiped with this song, God has begun to stir the importance of His Word washing over my life.

There is nothing like the presence of God. When you feel a touch from heaven coming down upon your life, you are forever changed. It is marvelous and too awesome to describe. Many times, I have felt God heal my heart with His touch. All I have to do is go to Him and get in a place of worship, and His healing presence will lift the cares off my life. I will be taken away in worship, and nothing else on earth matters during this worship experience. Many times, I have either seen or felt God's healing power touch my life and other people's lives—physically, emotionally and spiritually.

Some of these most powerful times have come while we have been in India. During various times of worship, my husband and I have seen God literally set captives free. For example, a few years ago, we partnered with worship leader Bob Fitts and watched God's power set a woman free from demonic oppression.

I remember this night vividly. We rode on a bus for several hours over rough roads and through intense traffic to reach the city where the worship concert was to be held. There are a billion people in India, so there can be as many as a million people in one city. In my hometown, a traffic jam occurs only when a large tractor or piece of equipment drives slowly through town. This is a small inconvenience compared to the masses of cars, scooters and bicycles on a single street in India.

There people drive in inches, not feet. I think they try to see if their cars can get close enough to kiss one another. I know it is a miracle when we drive safely in this nation because they seem to have their own set of traffic rules. All you need is a loud horn, and the biggest vehicle always has the right-of-way. I have even seen our driver reach out his window and pop a bicycle rider on the head because he wouldn't get out of the way fast enough. Needless to say, we could never get away with some of their driving antics.

After several hours of driving, we were more than thankful to arrive at our destination. There were no public rest stops, so unless we were willing to squat in a field, we held it until we reached our destination. This made for some hilarious situations on outreach.

Upon arrival, we freshened up and began to set up our sound equipment for a night of worship. After rehearsal, we joined to pray specifically for God to have His way in everyone's lives and to powerfully touch any area of anyone's life that needed healing.

On this particular night, I felt an uneasiness in my spirit. There seemed to be a resistance holding the people back from worshiping. As I looked over the audience of five hundred, it was as if I could feel their fears. They were literally afraid to enter into worship. I continued to pray during the worship, song after song. It felt as if we were coming up against some imaginary wall that needed to be broken down so that people could be set free to worship.

As Bob continued to usher in the presence of God through worship, a woman in the balcony started to scream violently because she was manifesting demonic oppression. It took several pastors to get her out of the concert hall, which left the crowd even more distracted than they were already.

In India, it is commonplace for someone to manifest a

demon because of all the different gods they serve. When people get saved and accept Jesus as Lord of their lives, they often are ostracized by their families. If someone converts from Islam or Hinduism to Christianity, many times there will be a contract put out to kill them. There is a great cost in the lives of these people when they find Jesus, but they are also the happiest people I know.

What took place next at this worship concert caused some commotion. Somehow, the woman who was manifesting a demon got loose and ran up on stage. There she spun one of our band members around and knocked over some microphones and cymbals as she tried to stop the concert. By that time, half a dozen pastors had run to our rescue. They took her out and cast the demon out of her. This all happened so fast we really didn't have time to react. We just kept worshiping God, with even more zeal and passion.

All the pastors laid hands on this woman and spoke the name of Jesus over her. Because there is so much power in His name, the demon had to flee. Light and darkness cannot mix, and so any fear I was experiencing came from the oppressive demonic spirits trying to keep the light of God's glory in worship from penetrating people's lives. Bob began to sing a song about not being afraid because the Lord washes away our fears.

At this point in the concert, the power of God showed up and washed away all the fear from the people's lives, including mine. We all traded in our fear for the joy of the Lord. It was an awesome exchange before our very eyes. Praise and worship went from the audience watching a concert to people's hands lifted high as God touched their lives with His incredible presence.

That is one of the best examples I can give of God's healing power touching the lives of people in a nation so full of darkness. Praise and worship hit the ceiling and exploded into vibrant praise that flowed out the doors and into the streets. As for the woman who was set free from demonic activity, she had no clue what she had done. Her spirit was set free to worship the One and only true God. It was a night we shall never forget.

On a more personal level, I want to share how God's healing power has washed over my life and the life of my church. As you read this chapter, open up your heart and ask the Lord to speak to you about His power washing over your life.

Recently, I was sitting outside asking the Lord to heal an area of my heart where I have experienced much hurt and pain. I have a terrible time sorting through my emotions after someone has spoken harsh words to me, such as a simple disagreement with a family member or harsh words from someone close to me who has misjudged my actions or my heart.

I believe one of the biggest tools of the enemy is to try to get us to speak shame over one another's lives. If he can use disagreements and fault-finding to keep us from walking in freedom, he will heap it upon our lives.

The enemy tries this with me. I have a tendency to want to run from the people who have offended me, and to be honest, I would rather not see the person again so I won't have to deal with the shame the situation caused. It is never easy to face our accusers.

I think most people can relate to these feelings. We all have been hurt by the words of family members or close friends or at work with our boss or co-workers. We can feel that no matter how well we perform, it is never quite good enough. Verbal abuse can occur while doing volunteer work, such as at your children's school or on the PTA or school board. There are many opportunities for divided interest among people over their children's education. I have seen how this can cause an uproar in a small community where everybody knows everybody. Almost everyone has a different opinion, and most are not willing to budge from their views.

As I was sitting on my porch that day, I was crying out to God to show me why it hurt me so much to be wounded by people's responses to me, why I felt these overwhelming emotions anytime someone said something bad to me.

God showed me a picture in my mind of my heart. I could visualize God holding my heart in His hands. He showed me all the recent flesh wounds that had penetrated my heart because of harsh words. In my mind, I watched as God took His finger and touched each flesh wound on my heart. Instantly, the healing touch of His hand removed the scars. Then God pointed to the bottom of my heart, where a deep hole had formed when I was a child. This hole had been caused by my dad speaking shame over me at different times in my life, including every time I was in the kitchen and never seemed to be able to do anything right. I always forgot to put something away or clean something off right away. And I can never remember my dad praising me for doing something right. Over the years, this caused a deep wound to be exposed in the depths of my heart.

What I saw next in this vision was God taking His entire hand and placing it over this deep hole. He left it there for a few moments, and when He removed His hand, the hole in my heart was gone, and the wounded heart had been exchanged for a beautiful, beating, red heart.

After God showed me this, I felt whole, complete and ready to love again. I sensed in my spirit that all these unkind words spoken over me had a purpose: God wanted to heal that big hole in my heart once and for all. He knew it would take a lot to get my attention, so He allowed situations in my life to bring the source of the pain in my heart to the surface. This was not an easy process, but it brought the deeper, hidden issue of shame to the light so I could see it for what it was. Then I was faced with the decision to make an exchange with the Lord. Ultimately, this set me free.

I had made another heart exchange with my Lord and Savior. Once again, God took my stony, unnatural, hardened heart, and He gave me a heart of flesh, sensitive again and responsive to the touch of God on my life. (See Ezekiel 11:19.)

However, I think the church is where the enemy likes to cause the greatest conflict. He knows that if he can get people to speak harsh words to one another, he can destroy friendships, unity and ultimately the church itself. This is what happened in my church when it split several years ago. All the accusations spoken over my pastor and my church just reflected people's differences and opinions. And yet the shame that was spoken caused much hurt and pain for everyone involved.

During this time, I can recall my pastor's response to all the offensive words. I remember him standing before the congregation soon after the church split and repenting for any part he had played in the split. He knew the scripture well that says, "He who covers *and* forgives an offense seeks love, but he who repeats *or* harps on a matter separates even close friends" (Prov. 17:9, AMP). Pastor Jon was taking the responsibility of a pastor and repenting for the areas in which he had failed. He knew the enemy was really the one who caused the split. He knew Satan would like nothing better than to destroy two pastors and a congregation full of friends.

As Pastor Jon broke down in tears, he could barely stand under all the shame spoken against him. But the power of God moved that day because he made an exchange with God, and through repentance and forgiveness, the shame he was under was removed. Pastor Jon also learned how to respond correctly and cover an offense with forgiveness and love.

We, too, need to know how to respond correctly to people after they have shamed us with their words, the way my pastor was able to and the way Jesus would have. I have found that the only way I can respond correctly is to go to my heavenly Father first and see what is going on inside my heart, as I did when He gave me the visions of my wounded heart healing.

Even after much healing and restoration over the course of my life, I have found that I need to continue to exchange the wounds of my heart for a clean heart time and again. The hardest part of receiving a clean heart is recognizing our desperate need for repentance. We must go to the Father daily and repent and be cleansed of our wrong heart and ask for God's forgiveness before we can ever come into His presence. Then we can stand clean before God and ask for His great and mighty power to lift us out of the bondage of shame.

Receiving a clean heart may be a process that all of us have to make the rest of our lives. To determine that, we have to turn to the Word of God.

In Psalm 51, King David cries out for God's forgiveness after committing adultery with Bathsheba and killing her husband to try to cover it up. King David was trying to hide the evidence against him instead of abiding in the Lord. He was called "a man after God's own heart," and yet here he is in need of repentance.

Many of us feel our sin and shame is just too big for God to forgive. We think that what we have done is too awful and too terrible for us to receive forgiveness. Well, no sin or shame is too big for our God to forgive if a heart is truly repentant and seeking forgiveness.

This is evident in King David's life. He was a man who fell into deep sin and shame. To regain his love relationship with the Lord, David had to make an exchange with God. King David's cries resound in Psalm 51:1–4: "O loving and kind God, have mercy. Have pity upon me and take away the awful stain of my transgressions. Oh, wash me, cleanse me from this guilt. Let me be pure again. For I admit my shameful deed—it haunts me day and night. It is against you and you alone I sinned, and did this terrible thing" (TLB).

David admitted that when he sinned, it was against the Lord. We, too, must confess that when we sin, it is against the Lord. Our sins might be of another nature: wrong or impure thoughts, wrong responses, immorality, theft or even a withholding of the places of shame in our lives from God.

But if we withhold any of our sins and shame from God it hurts others, ourselves and ultimately God. Sin and shame left untreated puts up walls blocking our relationships with others and with God.

When King David committed adultery, it immediately formed a wall in his love relationship with his heavenly Father. It also kept David from responding to others the way God would want him to respond, which resulted in the murder of Bathsheba's husband.

When we are hurt and wounded, we cannot respond to others correctly. If we can quickly come to the Father and turn over our broken hearts, He will in turn give us clean hearts. Then the enemy can no longer hold us captive, and we are free to move on and love others the way He would want them to be loved.

Therefore, we must take the time on a daily basis to cry out to God in repentance for a clean heart.

Whether we choose to repent or not, God sees it all. Nothing can be hidden from God. So when we try to cover up our shame and hide it from Him, it becomes sin. Since Jesus paid the highest price for all our sin and shame, doesn't He deserve every part of our lives—our hearts, our souls and our minds? Jesus made the ultimate exchange for every one of us, and He is desperately waiting for us to make clean heart exchanges. If King David can ask for God to create in him a clean heart and to renew in him a right spirit (see Psalm 51:10), don't you think we can come to the Father and ask Him for a clean heart and a right spirit?

This is my personal prayer each time I come to the Father. I must admit my shameful thoughts and deeds and ask for His forgiveness. When we are truly sorry for what we have done and we're willing to change, God can then wash over us by the power of His Word.

You may be thinking, *How can God's Word wash over my life?* The answer is in the Word:

> So that He might sanctify her, having cleansed her by the washing of water with the Word, that He might present the church to Himself in glorious splendor, without spot or wrinkle"
>
> —EPHESIANS 5:26–27, AMP

Paul is sharing how the water in baptism means the washing away of our sins. When Christ died for our sins, it was to wash over our lives and make us holy and clean. When we understand that the Word of God is alive and the breath of God inspired by the Holy Spirit, then we can feel the cleansing power of the Word in our lives. Jesus is trying to draw us to Him and build us up and make us strong.

He wants to be our covering, our protection, much like a loving husband protects his wife and family. This is stated in Ephesians 5:33: "So again I say, a man must love his wife as a part of himself; and the wife must see to it that she deeply respects her husband—obeying, praising and honoring him" (TLB). A covering is a type of protection and freedom, not a feeling of smothering or bondage. If you're not married, your covering here on earth could be your parents or someone you've allowed to be in authority over you, such as a pastor, elder or mentor.

Whoever they are, we must deeply respect those who are covering us. In John Bevere's book *Under Cover*, he scripturally describes what a covering is and says that those who stay under God's covering will find divine protection. For example, he writes: "Adam and Eve enjoyed freedom and protection in the garden under God's cover.

However, the moment they disobeyed, they found themselves in great need of the very thing they had voluntarily slipped out from under. . . it was the need, 'to cover themselves' (Gen. 3:7, NLT). Their disobedience to God's authority robbed mankind of the sweet freedom and protection they'd once known."

If we are being loved and served, deep respect comes easily to those who are covering us.

If we are being loved and served, deep respect comes easily to those who are covering us. If we are not being loved as Christ loved the church, it is a much harder set of circumstances. Then we need to ask God to help us respect our covering, even when it is undeserved. We must ask God to show us how to love and serve someone, even when it goes against our flesh. We get to honor those in authority over us, even when it is not merited.

I'll admit, before my dad was saved, it was not easy to honor and serve him. But earthly dads are a covering to us, even if they are not saved. God has placed them in authority over us. One particular time, I had to go to the heavenly Father and plead with Him to help me love, even when I was not being loved or covered as God intended.

I came home from my first year at Bible college filled with joy and passion for the Lord. When I arrived home, my dad had a friend living with him. Needless to say, I was upset with this arrangement. I felt a wide range of emotions—fear, anger, self-righteousness and resentment, to name a few. After several days had gone by, I finally had enough courage to confront my dad and let him know exactly how I felt. We got into a verbal knock-down, drag-out fight. There was a lot of yelling. I was hurt and angry because I didn't think my dad understood how I felt. I had come home that summer to work and have a great time with my dad, but here was this intruder in my home and my family life.

I remember crying and crying that day, asking the Lord what I should do to help this situation instead of complicate it. God told me to repent. In my mind, I was rationalizing why I was right. I was thinking, *Why should I repent when he is the one who is wrong?* God told me to turn the other cheek, go home and ask both my dad and his friend to forgive me. I think this was one of the hardest things I have ever done in my life. I really had to swallow my pride and my self-righteous attitude, and exchange them for humility, kindness and love. I had no idea how my dad would respond. All I could do was put my trust in the Lord and my life in His hands.

That night after work, I went into the living room and knelt by my dad's chair. I said, "Dad, I was wrong, and I'm sorry. Will you please forgive me for trying to tell you how to live your life? And Dad, this is your home, and you can have anybody you want to live here. I am so sorry for trying to tell you what you can and cannot do. Please forgive me." I also looked over at my dad's friend and asked him to forgive me. By this time, I had tears running down my face when I heard my dad say, "It's all right, sweetheart. I forgive you." Dad wasn't even saved yet, and by my turning the other cheek, my dad's heart melted in sweet love and compassion for his daughter. I left the room feeling much lighter, and I slept in complete peace that night.

When you learn to respect your covering and repent, God will wash over your life. When you admit you are wrong, even when you feel it is unjust, God will intervene on your behalf and move in people's hearts and lives. As I let God have His way with me, God then was able to have His way in my dad's life. My wrong response was no longer blocking the path to my dad's heart or holding back the process of God washing over his life. I had repented and made it right, and I had a clean heart before God. Then God was able to wash over my situation. He cleansed me from all the guilt and shame I was experiencing. He was making me pure, spotless and blameless again. Then He lifted me up and filled me with great joy. He filled me with compassion for my dad and his friend and overwhelmed me with His love. Then His grace and His glory streamed through my life and penetrated the darkness in my dad's life. My right response to my dad caused him to make an exchange with God that he didn't even understand yet.

My dad felt the unconditional love of Jesus in our living room that night, and it overwhelmed him to the point that he was able to make a right choice. I was the vessel God used to allow the Holy Spirit to come and move in my dad's heart and mind. This shows that even dads who don't know Jesus can make right choices when we love, honor and serve them.

The next day, when I got home from church, my dad had taken his friend somewhere, and he was never seen in our house again. God had intervened on my behalf. I understood what Isaiah meant.

> For I, the Lord, love justice; I hate robbery and wrong. I will faithfully reward my people for their

suffering and make an everlasting covenant with them.

—Isaiah 61:8, TLB

God will be faithful to reward those who suffer unjustly. He will settle all accounts. I was elated and filled with joy that God cared enough about me to rescue me from this difficult situation in my life. All I could do was weep as God's love washed over my life.

The rest of the summer, it was just me, my dad and Jesus. God was faithful to meet my needs, but only after I had honored my earthly father, who was my covering.

Many of you are in difficult situations now. If you are being physically abused, I would ask you to get help and let a pastor or elder be your covering. Many people who physically abuse others have been physically abused themselves. They have experienced so much shame and dishonor in their own lives that they can only give out shame and dishonor in the lives they touch.

You can be the vessel to see their lives changed forever. Pray and ask God what to do and how to love in difficult situations. Please seek help somewhere when there is physical abuse involved. Don't let it stay hidden. God sees your shame, and He knows how you have been dishonored. He wants to intervene in your life, just as He did in mine. He wants to wash over you by the power of His living, breathing Word.

My prayer for you is that your heart will be flooded with God's marvelous light, that you will be filled with compassion and overwhelmed by His great love. I pray that God's grace and glory will stream through your life like never before. I pray that the power of God's Word would wash over every area of your life.

Another example of God using the power of His Word to wash over people's lives is the special and unique relationship my church has with Bethel Gospel Assembly in Harlem. This has come about only by God uniting two churches for God's purpose and glory.

It happened on my first trip to New York City during my first experience at a worship weekend at Bethel Gospel Assembly. When Sunday came, my pastor was the first white pastor to preach at Bethel in a long time. Needless to say, we all stood out on that platform like Pillsbury Doughboys. Our team was so white among a sea of African-Americans. It felt odd to be the minority, surrounded by amazingly talented singers from their worship team, band and various choirs.

As my pastor began to share, he felt the urge to get a basin of water and wash that pastor's feet. So he motioned to one of the ushers to get him a basin of water. I am sure people were wondering what he was up to.

What took place next left the entire church speechless. As my pastor began to wash Bishop Ezra's feet, it was as if we were all getting our feet washed. Our pastor stood in the gap and repented for the sins of any white person who had ever wounded or inflicted pain on the lives of the people at Bethel. You could hear the sounds of the water splashing on the sides of the basin. You could feel the presence of God move. You could sense that God was about to wash over all of our lives. It was an undeniably awesome move of God.

Pastor Jon shared that he wished he could have washed all of their feet, but because Bethel is a large church, he said, "As I wash Bishop Ezra's feet, let it be a symbol that I am washing all of your feet." As my pastor obeyed the Holy Spirit's nudging, we watched as he humbly demonstrated God's Word and the power of it wash over an entire congregation. As God's power began to move, the people in the congregation began to weep, and walls began to fall between our white church from Oregon and their black church. We all got a fresh revelation of John 13:12–17, which shares the story of Jesus washing the disciples' feet before one of them betrayed him. After washing the disciples' feet, He instructs them to wash one another's feet. Jesus tells His disciples, "A servant is not greater than his master. Nor is the messenger more important than the one who sends him. You know these things—now do them!" (TLB).

I saw this scripture played out before my eyes. I am so glad to have a pastor who isn't afraid to do what he feels the Spirit of the Lord prompting him to do. To be a servant, he humbled himself and washed another brother's feet. In turn, Bishop Ezra washed my pastor's feet, and because of both of these servants' hearts, we have an incredible love relationship with many people from Bethel Gospel Assembly. I will never forget that day.

This is God's heart for the church across the world. To be able to understand what a true leader is, we must be humble enough to serve. We must serve God with everything within us and serve one another as Jesus ministered to us. Then God's amazing power and presence can wash over us and do incredible miracles right before our eyes—like the one at Bethel Gospel Assembly that day.

Putting two completely different churches with very different ethnic backgrounds together has to be a move of God. This was no coincidence. None of us could have dreamed this one up, let alone made it happen.

Bishop Ezra was willing to take a risk and let Pastor Jon share at Bethel. This opening has led to our churches joining together for God's glory time and again. For the last eight years, we have met in Oregon for our annual pastors conference. We have developed deep enduring friendships that have taken us all over the world together for outreach. Now hundreds of others join us at Christ's Center each year to celebrate the alliance we have formed with different churches across the United States and the world. We have a unique church indeed.

I believe this all happened because we had two pastors who were willing to humble themselves, pray, search for God and repent to each other. Then God heard from heaven and forgave our sins and healed our land. (See 2 Chronicles 7:14.) What an incredible promise to all of us in any walk of life. God wants to heal your land and your heart. He wants you to humble yourself and pray and turn from your sins. As you humble yourself, many times there is a need to ask for forgiveness. As you do, God will forgive you—but remember, God will only forgive you as you are able to forgive others.

> Be gentle and ready to forgive; never hold grudges. Remember, the Lord forgave you, so you must forgive others. Most of all, let love guide your life, for then the whole church will stay together in perfect harmony.
>
> —COLOSSIANS 3:13–14, TLB

As you forgive others, pray blessings over their lives. You cannot hold grudges against people if you are praying for the blessings of the Lord upon their lives.

This is when God's glory can fall upon our lives. He

will lift us up and use each of us to shine His glory for all the world to see. This is when unity takes place between churches, races and people. God's glory will touch our lives when we walk in love, accepting one another's differences or preferences and forgiving one another as Christ has forgiven us.

It is my prayer that you will allow God's Word to wash over your life just like the waters covering the sea. (See Isaiah 11:9.) In the same way the power of waves break onto the shoreline, allow the power of the truths in God's Holy Word cover you with the knowledge of the Lord.

> The time will come when all the earth is filled, as the waters fill the sea, with an awareness of the glory of the Lord.
>
> —HABAKKUK 2:14, TLB

I believe at this time, many people shall see God's glory and return to the Lord. People from every tongue, tribe and nation will rise up and worship the One and only true God. As this event unfolds, God will provide an escape for His people, an exchange, if you may.

It will be the ultimate exchange, when the trumpet sounds and we see the Lord sitting upon His throne, high and lifted up, and our response will be, "Holy, holy, holy is the Lord of Hosts; the whole earth is filled with his glory." (Isa. 6:3, TLB). During this time on earth, only God's people will make this final exchange. God clearly knows who His chosen people are. When the day of God's wrath is at hand, no one will escape it except those who have exchanged their old lives for new ones.

Because of the shed blood of Jesus, we have open access on a daily basis to enter into the presence of God.

We can approach God boldly. But for the unrepentant sinner, there is no escape from the judgment of the Lord.

Therefore, I am begging you today to make this ultimate exchange with the Lord. Please open yourself up to exchanging your old, hardened heart for a new, soft, pliable heart. All you need to do is pray this prayer with me:

> *Lord, please forgive me for my sins and come into my heart. I want to give up my old life in exchange for a new life. I want to trade in my stony heart for a soft, responsive heart. Lord, please take this shame off my life and exchange it for Your glory. Lord, I love You, and I want to know everything there is to know about You. I confess that I am a sinner, and I accept You as the Lord of every area in my life. Amen.*

ELEVEN

Pressing On

All of us are in a race called *life*. As Christians, we should have one goal in mind: to reach the finish line and receive the prize, which is eternity in heaven. What matters most to the Lord is how we run the daily race He has called us to run so we can accomplish what He is asking us to do. Now that we know the importance and potential of God washing over our lives, we must seek this each and every day as we press on toward the finish line.

What does *press on* mean? It means "to urge on, to strive for eagerly, to persist no matter what our circumstances are or what people think of us." To apply pressure to something means to exert force on a person or set of circumstances, which will propel action to the individual or situation in spite of any resistance.

A Christian pressing through life is like a runner pressing through a race. When I line up for a race with hundreds of runners, I am always amazed by all the excitement and anticipation among everyone waiting for the gun to go off. Runners bristle with nervous energy as they stretch their muscles, exchange running stories and make that last trip to the bathroom before the race begins. Then all the pent-up adrenaline is released as the gun goes off and the runners begin their race with the hopes of finishing strong.

If runners start out too fast, they will go into oxygen debt and their lungs will burn, and some will have to slow down or even walk to be able to cross the finish line.

Experienced runners pace themselves with their watch and hold back a little early on so they can finish strong. Trained runners never lose sight of the finish line. They always know when to pick up the pace and press even harder to cross the finish line at a respectable time. A disciplined runner always has a goal in mind.

Similarly, as Christians, we must learn to train and pace ourselves so we'll be able complete the race that God has called each of us to run. If we start out too fast in our lives, we'll get ahead of God, and He will pull back on the reigns and slow us down. If we're the type of people who hesitate and drag their feet a little, God may allow something or someone to come along and help jump start us to get us going a little faster.

In the Bible, Paul is one who pressed through life.

> I don't mean to say I am perfect. I haven't learned all
> I should even yet, but I keep working toward that day

when I will finally be all that Christ saved me for and wants me to be. No, dear brothers, I am still not all I should be but I am bringing all my energies to bear on this one thing: Forgetting the past and looking forward to what lies ahead, I strain to reach the end of the race and receive the prize for which God is calling us up to heaven because of what Christ Jesus did for us.

—PHILIPPIANS 3:12–14, TLB

Like Paul, none of us can say we have "arrived" yet. We haven't learned all we need to know about God, and I believe that throughout eternity, we will be students of the most high God. We must determine that our purpose in life is to become more intimately and personally acquainted with our Lord and Savior on a daily basis. To be able to know who we are, what we're to put our hand to, and why we need to do it, we must begin to perceive, recognize and understand the wonders and ways of Jesus.

To be able to lay hold of all that God has for us, we must learn to press through our past, to the present, which will determine our future. Our past is not our future. God is the great "I Am." He is the beginning and the end. He will complete the work He has started in each of us, as long as we're ready to let go of our past and press on toward our future.

When I have to press through something, most of the time it is not an easy process, although I think it could be. Many times, my problems are much smaller than how blown up they become in my mind. If I would only take my eyes off my circumstances and look to Jesus, the problem that seemed like a major issue would seem quite minor.

When I go to India to minister, I must press through

my fear of flying just to be able to get on an airplane. I have learned to hide God's Word in my heart so that when I am afraid, I can quote the Word. I know that His perfect love cast out all fear; therefore, if I concentrate on how much my heavenly Father loves me and how He feels about me, the fear will leave, and it will have no control over me.

More pressing comes after I arrive in India. It is a completely different world over there compared to my comfortable little grass seed farm. Just the new sights, constant sounds and different scents were overwhelming to my senses.

Once again, I have to press into my relationship with Jesus to find peace when I am out of my comfort zone. Many times, I've had others stand and pray with me over my fears. It isn't wrong to have others stand in the gap in prayer for you when you are facing trying circumstances or trials. In fact, it is a biblical principle to have someone standing on the right and left of you during battles. For example, Moses let Aaron and Hur hold up his arms in prayer to ensure victory over the Amalekites. (See Exodus 17:10–13.) This battle was won because three men knew the importance of prayer, intercession and worship.

Another example of pressing into a relationship with Jesus to find peace is in the familiar Bible story in Daniel 3:1–30. Three young Jewish men of prayer, Shadrach, Meshach and Abednego, were tested and strengthened by injustice. They were out of their comfort zones because they were away from their homeland; they were different, set apart, from all the other people serving the king. But they were raised to stand their ground in their relationship with God, no matter what their circumstances dictated.

In this story, the king commanded them to bow down to his idol. When they refused to bow down, it made the king so mad that he threatened to throw them into a fiery furnace to be burned alive. Now, if I knew I would be burned alive because of a set of circumstances, my human side tells me to run from danger and not stand and face my accusers.

The king gave the three men one more chance to bow down, but again they refused and stayed true to God and their beliefs. They didn't hesitate for one minute to put their lives in the hands of God. They had enough faith to believe their God would deliver them.

This made the king so violently angry that he had the furnace heated up seven times hotter. The enemy was trying to pressure the men into bowing down to the idols of the land. Satan knew that if he could get them to compromise their faith, they would be stuck and held powerless over their situation.

As they held firm and refused to bow down, they were thrown into the fiery furnace, and the fire was so hot that it killed the men who threw them into the furnace.

What took place next was an incredible miracle of God. The three men didn't know whether God would rescue them. But He did, and they were untouched by the fire. Not a hair on their heads was singed. They didn't even smell like smoke. Only the ropes that bound them had been burned.

We as Christians need to wake up and grasp hold of the awesome magnitude of power that God used to set the captives free. If Shadrach, Meshach and Abednego could believe that God would rescue them out of their horrific situation, can we not trust that our God will intervene on our behalf, no matter what our circumstances might be?

These men made a stand for God on the principle of integrity. They vowed to stand up for what they believed in, regardless of what could happen to them.

What would you do? In what areas of your life are you already bowing down to idols of distraction? Do you stand up for what you believe in, even when your circumstances get seven times harder? Or do you run and hide from conflict? I believe most of us who believe in God would quickly say, "I would never bow down and deny my God." However, you may already be doing so.

For me, it might be eating that extra piece of cake and not denying my flesh. For others, it might be watching a movie or television program that is too violent or sexually graphic. Anytime we bow down to the things of this world instead of denying our flesh, we bow down to the enemy's tricks by using worldly temptations put in place to distract our lives and hold us captive. As you pass by that yummy piece of chocolate cake just beckoning you to eat it, you may rationalize, *I'll only take one little bite*, and before you know it, you've eaten the entire piece. When we give in to our flesh, we don't like to acknowledge this as idol worship.

So now if you think you may give in to idol worship, you should be ecstatic to know that nothing—not even fleshly temptations—can bind us when God wants to set us free. The same power that delivered the three Jewish men from the fiery pit raised Christ from the dead and is available now to rescue us from our temptations and circumstances. There are eternal reasons for our temporary trials. If we can overcome them, they make our character more Christlike.

King Nebuchadnezzar is astounded by this divine intervention of God, and shares with the people.

> "Blessed be the God of Shadrach, Meshach, and Abednego, for he sent his angel to deliver his trusting servants when they defied the king's commandment, and were willing to die rather than serve or worship any god except their own. Therefore, I make this decree, that any person of any nation, language, or religion who speaks a word against the God of Shadrach, Meshach, and Abednego shall be torn limb from limb and his house knocked into a heap of rubble. For no other God can do what this one does." Then the king gave promotions to Shadrach, Meshach, and Abednego, so that they prospered greatly there in the province of Babylon.
>
> —DANIEL 3:28–30, TLB

Because Shadrach, Meshach, and Abednego were men of integrity, they were rescued, God's name was proclaimed as the One true God throughout the nation, they were blessed for their faithfulness, and they prospered greatly.

I want to have the kind of faith these men had. I want to stand up for my God no matter what my circumstances may be. I want to see the miracles of God in my life and be rescued out of my fiery furnace. God's double portion comes to those who have the guts to stand up for what they believe and the faith to face their enemies, no matter what.

Too many of us give excuses, such as, "It's too hard, I can't do this," or, "I'll only bow down this one time, and I really won't mean it in my heart." We rationalize, "I'll only go to this movie just this once because my friend who is lonely wants me to go." Or we might use excuses that the three Jewish men could have used, "God knows what's in my heart, and it's the king who has power over us, so we better bow down." "God will excuse us this time." "We're on foreign land". "This isn't my home, so it doesn't really matter, right?"

What are some of the excuses you might use when pressures or conflict come into your life? In what areas do you compromise and conform to the world?

Many times, distractions seem small until they become strongholds in our minds. For example, before I became a Christian, I listened to worldly music. I have a gift of memorizing lyrics easily. I still can probably sing all the hit songs that were popular before 1980. After I stopped listening to secular music, I realized that music has the power to shape the mind, will and emotions. Oftentimes, it is what we see or hear that causes us to compromise our standards. When we let our guard down even one time, it opens the door and makes it easier to settle for less the next time.

Now, instead of feeling discouraged or depressed because of a sad song, I am constantly lifted up in my spirit because I listen to praise and worship music. I challenge you to give up listening to secular music and exchange it for listening to Christian music. Even if you only do it for a week or a month, you'll soon find your mind being renewed and uplifted, instead of torn down and discouraged. Now that is a great exchange.

The world has taken hold of our senses and violated them. The movies I was allowed to watch as a child seem so boring compared to the thrill and excitement in motion pictures today. As a parent of three children, I am conservative when it comes to what I allow my children to watch. I don't care if I'm the bad guy because I know that what my children see with their eyes will produce fruit, good or bad. It only takes one little seed to be planted into their minds to distract them from Godly principles and into worldly pleasures.

The same is true with adults. Just because we're older, more mature and more able to reign in our flesh doesn't mean we cannot be lured into watching things we shouldn't. We, too, must be on constant alert as to what is affecting our mind, will and emotions. We must be diligently aware of what we need to stand up for when it comes to what we see and hear.

When I'm struggling with worldly pressures, people or circumstances, I can easily get caught up in them until the enemy has wound me up tighter than a top. During this period, sometimes I have trouble sleeping, my stomach is in knots, and I respond wrong to others. God will allow me to try to take charge of my circumstances, even try to fix them, until I am utterly exhausted and lying at His feet in deep repentance.

Then through the sweetness of His Spirit, my heavenly Father picks me up and holds me close in His loving arms and nourishes me back to Himself. Isaiah 40:11 paints this picture: "He will feed His flock like a shepherd; He will gather the lambs in His arm, He will carry them in His bosom and will gently lead those that have their young" (AMP).

After I have spent this intimate time of repentance with my shepherd, then I can run along into the Word, and God will breathe life into my situation. I can press on toward the finish line.

Second Corinthians 4:8–9 illustrates the principle of moving forward and not giving up: "We are pressed on every side by troubles, but not crushed and broken. We are perplexed because we don't know why things happen as they do, but we don't give up and quit. We are hunted down, but God never abandons us. We get knocked down, but we get up again and keep going" (TLB).

What a great exchange. We may feel pressed on every side from the things of this world, but we are never crushed. We may be persecuted by others, but we are never deserted. We may be struck down and hurt, but we are never destroyed. What promises await those who are faithful to the One and only King of kings.

Also, as a marathon runner, I have learned to press through many miles during good and bad days. On good days, it's easy to run and finish my miles with a smile on my face, as I feel a sense of accomplishment. On bad days, it's hard even to get myself out the door and begin to run. Those are the days I have learned to press through my mind, will and emotions and go for a run anyway.

Another example of pressing on amid pressure is when you squeeze oranges to make fresh juice. You must put lots of pressure on the oranges so they will turn into juice. It takes many oranges to make just one full glass of freshly squeezed juice. There is a cost involved, but the taste of freshly squeezed orange juice makes it worthwhile. Another benefit is that fresh and genuine products have more nutritious value compared to canned and artificial products.

The same principle applies when we press through our past. We will face bad days. We may feel squeezed. It might be hard to confront our fears and face our past. But the results are worth any amount of pressure used to free us from our past and any pain involved in the process.

Personally, I can now say that God has more than doubly paid me back for any hardship or injustice in my life.

I wasn't able to say that twenty-five years ago, when my family life was a disaster. But because I have allowed God to put pressure on the shame of my past, I am now walking in freedom and experiencing joy from the light of His glory.

Furthermore, whatever price I have had to pay to get free is nothing compared to the price Jesus paid for all our sins and shame so we could walk freely and reflect His glory in our lives.

To press through our past we must be willing to give up control, or the tension of our past will overtake and overwhelm us. A few adjectives that describe control are domineering, browbeating, bullying, oppressive, restrained and reserved.

Being in control means being in the driver's seat, doing all the steering and choosing—deciding—whether to go to the right or to the left on any given day. Being in control of your destiny means that you have the power of authority in your life. You are the one directing your life's course.

When people maintain control, they are taking the place of God in their lives. The things in their past may have been so dysfunctional that the only way they know how to survive is to be in charge and not let anyone else, or any circumstance, have control. I know. I was one of them.

For example, when my parents divorced, it was out of my control, so I decided that they could make their own mistakes, but that I was going to succeed in life and be a winner. I was going to be somebody. Their wrong choices were not going to defeat me or stop me from being triumphant. As those who have been shamed in the past try to control their future, I was taking control of my life.

The only way I know how to relinquish control is to let God have total control of all areas of my life. There must be an exchange with God over who is in charge. To have freedom in our lives, He must be Lord of every area. Kay Arthur gives a great definition of *lordship*: "His total possession of me and my total submission to Him as Lord and Master."

To be able to receive blessings from God, you must make these life-changing exchanges. You have to give God your shame in order to receive his double portion of blessings on your life. It is much like the exchange that takes place when you go to a restaurant. You give money, and the waiter gives you food. If there is no monetary exchange, there will be no food exchange.

If I want the blessings of God on my life, I must sow good seeds to be able to reap the benefits. If I never sow or if I sow bad seeds, the blessings of God will be withheld from my life. When I sow good seeds into someone's life, God instantly will put His hand of blessing and anointing on my life. What an awesome exchange! However, if I withhold even one part of my life from God, I will continue to stay stuck and not reap all the blessings and benefits God has for me.

Just as God heaped a double portion on the lives of Shadrach, Meshach and Abednego when they gave Him total control, He wants to do this for all of us. We must be willing to give up our lives so we can truly be saved, redeemed, rescued and blessed.

This is stated in Matthew 16:25: "For whoever is bent on saving his [temporal] life [his comfort and security here] shall lose it [eternal life]; and whoever loses his life [his comfort and security here] for My sake shall find it [life everlasting]" (AMP).

To let go of the control that our past has over us, we

must release the pressure mounting against us. We all have internal gauges to let us know when we have had enough of the pressure.

It's similar with car gauges that signal the driver when something isn't working properly. If a car is losing too much water, it will overheat. As the car gets hot, the gauge light will go on, and steam will begin to flow from the engine. If a driver respects what the gauges are telling him, he will pull over and deal with the problem. If the driver is careless and keeps going no matter what the gauges say, his engine could blow up.

When we are dealing with our past having control over us, we can either pay attention to God's nudging and giving warnings to us and check our lives, or we can keep going in our own strength until we are exhausted and spent with nothing left to give.

When we reach this point, we're ready to give up control and cry out to God for help. At this desperate threshold in our lives, we are at the best place we can be. We are out of control, at the bottom, at the end of ourselves, with nothing left to do but to surrender. Then healing can come.

We've done all we can, and now it's time to release control of our lives to God and to let Him do the rest. This is the place where He longs for us to be.

Then, because light penetrates darkness, as we turn over the shame of control over our lives to God, we walk in the freedom found in the light of His glory. However, if we don't confess that we've lived our lives full of control and bring it out into the open and reveal it to God, His light cannot shine upon our shame and release us from the grip of darkness in our past.

The moment we surrender control of our situation to Him is the moment He can begin to work on our behalf. What a great exchange. The pressure of being in control is gone, and now He is able to open our eyes so we can see the direction for our lives. Then He will fulfill our dreams according to His plans, not ours. (See Jeremiah 29:11–14.)

Releasing control may sound simple, but it is complicated to try to apply it to our lives and put actions with our words. That's because we tend to like things in nice, neat little packages. We all like to do things our way, and we wish everyone would just comply with our wishes.

We don't really care to be out of our comfort zones, so we control the environment around us to feel safe and comfortable. When we do this, oftentimes we are not only controlling our own lives, but the lives of those around us.

I struggle with this. Before I can leave my house in the morning, I like everything to be neat and tidy and in place. I like the beds to be made, the laundry started and all the dishes put in the dishwasher. If you have children, this can easily upset the flow of an entire morning.

Someone always forgets to put his or her dishes away or clothes in the laundry, or at the last minute, someone needs something for school that he or she forgot to tell me about until morning. Then you must squeeze in the time to stop at the store and pick up that item. By the time I've dropped my children off at school, my nice, neat, uncomplicated morning has gotten out of my control fast.

I can choose to respond in two ways. One way is to go with the flow and leave the house a mess because it will be there when I return. Or I can raise the energy level in the house by rushing everyone so my house is left the way I like it.

The relaxed way results in peace; the intense way causes stress and even can inflict shame on someone. I have learned that I have to give up my control over some areas so we all can have peaceful mornings.

This has not been easy for me to do. I still prefer things to be tidy, and my flesh likes to get my way when things are left undone. I can do more harm than good if I verbally shame my children just so my home is left the way I like it.

A biblical example of someone in extreme control of his life is Paul, formerly called Saul. He had a past filled with malice and hatred for anyone professing to be a believer in Christ. When he was in control of his life, he charged others to destroy Christians.

Paul was the one who held the coats of those who martyred the first Christians (Acts 7:57–58). Yet despite Paul's violent ways, God chose to exchange his past for a future filled with giving the hope of the Gospel away to many. (See Acts 9.) As Paul says in Philippians 4:13, we all would like to forget about our past and look forward to the future.

Even if our past is filled with sin and shame as was Paul's, God can remove that from our lives "As far away from us as the east is from the west" (Ps. 103:12, TLB). God loves to use broken people who have come out of lives filled with sin and shame to reflect His glory to lost people.

I like to call people who have been brought out of shame "reflectors of God's glory." We are to be "mirrors" that shine the image of Jesus wherever we go and whatever we do.

When we receive Jesus into our hearts, the reflection

we see of ourselves in a mirror changes because now we are reflecting the image and character of God.

Paul describes the beauty of this in 2 Corinthians 2:14: "For through what Christ has done, he has triumphed over us so that now wherever we go he uses us to tell others about the Lord and to spread the Gospel like a sweet perfume" (TLB).

When we are a reflection of God's glory, people cannot help but take notice. Our lives will be a sweet, wholesome fragrance releasing an aroma both to the saved and the unsaved. We hold the fragrance of Christ within us. Just as Jesus became a sweet-smelling aroma of sacrifice to God on our behalf, so are we a sweet perfume to the broken, dying people of this world.

Since we always will be changing from "glory to glory," we must keep working toward being all that Jesus has saved us for and called us to be. We must press on. And this includes being loved and loving others in return.

God started developing our specific purposes within us while we were young children. When I was six I began taking piano lessons, which developed in me a heart to sing and worship. Although at that age I never thought of going to India and training up young men and women to be worshipers, God already had planted in me a heart to love Him through worship and to give that passion away to others by my example of expressive worship.

As he uses me, God's plan is to use all of His people to be vessels of love so the lost and dying people on this earth will turn their hearts toward heaven and begin to love the One and only King of kings. If each of us did our part to bring healing to the broken heart of God by loving these people, then God would bring healing to our land,

and we would be one nation under God once again.

One of the things that keeps us from loving God and loving people is the shame from our past. For example, my mom's affair and my dad's secret homosexual lifestyle when they were going through their divorce caused me suffering that kept me tightly wrapped in the pain of my past. No matter how hard I tried, I couldn't get rid of all the emptiness, anger and pain I was feeling until I exchanged my past for an incredible future with Jesus.

Many of us live in our past hurts, failures and disappointments, and that keeps us from pressing on and being all that God has created us to be. Some of us will even live in the past because those were the "good ole days." We say things such as, "I sure wish things were the way they used to be."

But we are not supposed to get stuck in our past. When God brings up things from our past, it is to unleash His healing power of love in our lives. God wants us to deal with our past and bring revelation into our lives so that any lie of the enemy will be exposed and brought to light.

If we keep looking and thinking about the past, we will have opportunities to return to it. And when we return to it, we miss the blessings of God and the wonderful life God has for us.

This happened to Lot's wife (see Genesis 19:26). She looked back and became a pillar of salt. Looking back at her past brought on the destruction of her future. Her heart still wanted the past. She was not willing to ask God to change her heart. She desired her past, and it was full of sin. In other words, she desired her sins more than she wanted to press forward into all that God had for her.

This happens to many of us, too. We don't want to

give up this or that. We are an undisciplined nation with selfish hearts and desires. God wants us to strip off anything that would slow us down or hold us back, especially those sins that wrap themselves tightly around our feet and trip us up.

> Let us run with patience the particular race that God has set before us. Keep your eyes on Jesus, our leader and instructor. He was willing to die a shameful death on the cross because of the joy he knew would be His afterwards; and now he sits in the place of honor by the throne of God.
>
> —HEBREWS 12:1–2, TLB

So jump in and let God have His way with your life. Don't withhold one more ounce of your past from Him. He knows about it anyway. We must strip away everything that could slow us down or trip us up.

If we are constantly looking back to our past, we cannot keep our eyes on Jesus.

Isaiah 43:18–19 tells us to forget about our past: "Do not [earnestly] remember the former things; neither consider the things of old. Behold I am doing a new thing! Now it springs forth; do you not perceive *and* know it *and* will you not give heed to it? I will even make a way in the wilderness and rivers in the desert" (AMP).

God wants to do a new thing in our lives. When we press forward we can run with patience the race that God has called us to run

God does not hold us in bondage, and neither do people. Satan, our enemy, is the one who wants us living in the shame of our past and not moving forward. If he can keep us there, or even in the successes of our past, Satan has done his job, and we have given him victory over our lives. When this happens, we are the ones blocking our own freedom.

We hold the keys to freedom in our hands. When God sent Jesus to die on the cross for our sin and shame, this single, unselfish act of love broke through the bondage of our past, which sets us free and releases us to run again.

John 8:36 says, "So if the Son liberates you [makes you free men], then you are really *and* unquestionably free" (AMP). It is the truth in God's awesome Word that sets us free.

Do you want to run the race that Jesus has set before you? The choice is yours. There is a cost, and yet the cost will set you free and give you eternal rewards. God's exchange rate is always a double portion. You cannot lose if you surrender every part of your life to Him. Please take a moment and pray this prayer with me:

> *Dear Jesus, please forgive me for withholding any part of my life from You. I surrender my past, my present and my future. I give You my discarded dreams, my broken past, and I ask You to come heal my shattered life. I want You to have total control over every aspect of my life. Lord, I give You my heart, my soul, my mind and all my strength. I realize now that You are Lord, and I turn my life over to you. I place You in the driver's seat, and I will try my best not to be a back-seat driver. Lord, wherever You lead me, I will follow to the right or to the left. Please keep me under the shadow of Your mighty wings. Lord, I understand Isaiah 40:31, which says, "But they that wait upon the Lord shall renew their strength. They shall mount up with wings like eagles; they shall run and not be weary; they shall walk and*

not faint" (TLB). Oh God, teach me how to wait on You and Your timing so I can see revival and resurrected life come to pass over my life and over the life of my country.

TWELVE

Send Revival

If you could build a house for God, what kind of house would you build? What kind of house do you think God is looking for? Would God's house be large or small? Would it be made simply of wood or expensive brick with exquisite marble? Would the entryway be designed with pillars to showcase the home, or would huge, ornate doors impress all who enter? Would God's house be white and have a picket fence, or would it be painted green to be the envy of all others? Or is God looking for another type of house? Whatever the type, how could you ever build a house grand enough for God?

He deserves the best—and not just in a house. But He doesn't always get it.

This is evident when the prophet Haggai asks, "Is it then the right time for you to live in luxurious homes, when the Temple lies in ruins?" (Haggai 1:4, TLB). The temple is a symbol of our relationship with God, and it lies unfinished. The Lord wants us to rebuild it. He is calling us to get our priorities in order. Our number one priority should be building on our relationship with Jesus.

But before this building can begin, like all reconstruction jobs, they need an architect and blue prints. Decisions have to be made about the design and layout of the house, of course, but the most important decision is who the builder will be. Without a good builder, your house could end up looking like a bad remodeling job instead of a new house.

Isaiah identifies the type of builder God is looking for:

> Thus says the Lord: 'Heaven is My throne, and the earth is My footstool. What kind of house would you build for Me? And what kind can be My resting-place? For all these things My hand has made, and so all these things have come into being [by and for Me], says the Lord. But this is the man to whom I will look and have regard; he who is humble and of a broken or wounded spirit, and who trembles at My word and reveres My commands."
> —ISAIAH 66:1–2 , AMP

He is searching to and fro for a remnant of God's chosen people who are humble enough to repent, who are broken enough over their lifestyles to turn from them and return to God, who are wounded and yet not bitter from life's circumstances so that God can remove their sin and shame and exchange them for His amazing Glory.

Then all who make this exchange will reap the blessings

filled with great times of refreshment and revival coming from the very presence of God. (See Acts 3:19.)

If we put God first, He will bless our lives and fulfill our deepest longings. However, if we put God in any other place, all our efforts will be in vain, and we will miss out on the genuine blessings that God wants to shower on us. The harder we work to get ahead in this world, the less we will have because we are ignoring our spiritual lives.

We may plant much through all we do in life, but we will harvest little because God isn't number one in our lives. We may have lots of material possessions, but these things will not ultimately satisfy us. At first, having nice things seems to make us happy, but in the end, we will always be left with feelings of longing for something to fulfill the emptiness that resides deep within us.

Where do you put all your efforts? Into your beautiful home? Things you like to do? Or your relationship with God? What takes first place in your life?

God has waited so long for someone to rebuild His temple. He promises in Haggai 1:8 that when we rebuild His temple, He will be pleased with it and appear there in all His glory. There has been a drought in our lives because His temple lies in ruin. God is holding back the rain, and the only way a monsoon will come in our lives is if we worship the Lord with everything within us and hold nothing back. (See Haggai 1:12.) We must exchange our self-absorbed attitudes for a renewed passion to worship God. God will give us the desire to rebuild His temple, but we must put action to our words before we can begin the rebuilding process.

Have you ever waited a long time for something to

come? I mean, really waited, months, sometimes years? Sometimes it feels as if what we are waiting for will never come. But when it does, refreshment comes to your soul—much like an ocean breeze around you—formed by the waves of life.

This is how God feels about His temple. He has been waiting so long for His people to begin rebuilding their lives centered around His, so He can pour out His glory upon "the church." This is when we grow in leaps and bounds, and it is only then that God can reap a harvest from our lives.

It is much like when spring comes. Winter can be bare and cold and wet, and sometimes it feels as if I may never see the sunshine again. But when the sun finally comes out, and those warm rays peek between the clouds, I know I have made it through the storms of winter. The moment those first daffodils pop through the hard earth and begin budding brilliant yellow flowers, I know that all the hard work enduring winter has been worth it.

It is just like our incredible relationship with God the Father and His Son, Jesus. He gave us the free gift of salvation; it cost Jesus His life, and all it costs us is a desire to repent of our sins and surrender our lives completely to Him.

When God created us, He knew exactly who we could be and how we could affect the world around us. But like a seed planted into the ground, our lives must be firmly planted before they can produce a harvest. But before we can be planted, our ground, our lives, may have to be plowed over and over again.

My husband, Mark, is a third-generation grass seed farmer. He learned how to farm from his dad, just like his dad learned from his father. The quality of equipment has improved greatly, but the technique of farming remains similar.

When Mark prepares a field for planting, he begins by plowing up the ground. Then he takes a big piece of equipment called a roller and goes over the ground again and again. This smashes the dirt clods to make the ground smooth for planting.

This is much like what God does in our lives. He will till up our past, only so he can heal all our pain, so our lives will really begin to grow and blossom.

As a field is prepared and planted, the sun and the rain will make the seed grow so it will produce a harvest. Similarly, if we plant the Word in our hearts, fresh revelation will come and transform us from our old ways of doing things to new ways. We will be changing from "glory to glory."

Somewhere along the way, Mark will have to fertilize the ground, and he may even have to spray for bugs. If he doesn't do these things at just the right time, he could lose part of the harvest he planted. Similarly, in our relationship with Jesus, the more we invest, the greater the exchange and the higher the return on our investment.

My husband tends our grass seed fields with care. Spring comes, and I know the fields will begin to grow and that harvest time is near. If Mark has done a good job and has been obedient and disciplined to do all he needs to do, God will do His part, and a harvest will come. On the other hand, if Mark were a lazy farmer and decided not to fertilize or spray, our harvest might become infested with bugs, or our grass seed may produce only half as much as it should under the watchful eye of a good farmer.

As with our love relationship with Jesus, the investment we make determines the kind of return we will receive. Therefore, we must place a higher priority on our relationship with Jesus. He must be more important to us than anyone or anything in the world. We must even place Him above our own personal comfort. When we stretch beyond our comfort zone, it prompts us to draw near to Jesus. If we draw near to Him, He will draw nearer still. Now that is a great exchange!

> Jesus said to them, My food (nourishment) is to do the will of Him Who sent Me and to accomplish *and* completely finish His work. Do you not say, It is still four months until harvest time comes: Look! I tell you, raise your eyes and observe the fields *and* see how they are already white for harvesting. Already the reaper is getting his wages [he who does the cutting now has his reward], for he is gathering fruit [crop] unto life eternal, so that he who does the planting and he who does the reaping may rejoice together. For in this the saying holds true, One sows and another reaps. I sent you to reap a crop for which you have not toiled. Other men have labored and you have stepped in to reap the results of their work.
> —JOHN 4:34–38, AMP

We are fed by doing God's will for our lives and by completing the work He already has started. We are nourished not only by what we take in from Jesus, but also by what we give out to minister to the needs of others.

An example is that as I study and read God's Word for my own personal growth and enjoyment, I reap the benefits of God speaking to me through His powerful Word. But it takes two to be in a relationship. Therefore, when

God speaks to me, I must then respond and act on what He is saying to me.

When I began writing this book, it was out of an act of obedience to what I felt God was speaking into my life at that time. Now, as I come to the close of this book, I know that I will reap a harvest for the seeds I have planted in the lives of my readers, whose lives will be transformed by making shame exchanges.

There is a continual harvest ready to be reaped. Millions of people are broken and hurting and in need of a Savior. Look around, and you will find people ready and waiting to hear about the love of Jesus.

This happened in a big way after the World Trade Center was destroyed. People all over were literally lined up, ready to hear about the love and comfort found only in Jesus. Our false sense of security was ripped out from under us. The only true source of security people could find was Jesus.

During this time, my home church on the West Coast prayed for our Alliance church in Harlem, on the East Coast. We heard reports of people streaming through that church wanting prayer. For years, people have sown into that ministry, called Bethel Gospel Assembly, and now it's time to reap the harvest. New Yorkers will never be the same again—and neither shall we.

One person sows, and someone else comes along and reaps the benefits... Yet they all rejoice. We got to pray for our brothers and sisters from Bethel Gospel Assembly. They got to put their physical arms around people and walk them through their hurt, shock and grief. They also got to feed and provide beds for hundreds of people working at Ground Zero.

We worked for Christ through prayer, while our friends labored by literally showing love. Their reward was seeing the harvest of souls. The sower sees the seed; the reaper sees the reward of the harvest.

If we humble ourselves and are broken before the Lord, He will pick us up and make His face to shine upon our lives; but we must be empty of ourselves and broken to the point that all we want and need is our Savior. More than ever, at this time, people are desperate, humble and broken enough that they are willing to admit their desperate need for a Savior.

What does it mean to be humble and broken? It means that we have come to a place in our lives where we have nothing left. We have hit bottom. We are at the end of ourselves. We engage in no more self-centered living. We have no more selfish ambitions or motives. We ask no more questions such as, *"What about me?"* Then and only then can His mighty hand come and lift us up and restore our hearts. God lifts up the humble, but turns His face from the proud and haughty.

Those who fear the Lord stand in awe and give glory to the Lord for everything in their lives. They take no credit for anything they have done or any successes they have achieved. They recognize that the Lord is their all in all, and everything they are and even the air they breathe come from their Creator.

Our response should be much like that of Jesus' mother, Mary.

> For he, the mighty Holy One, has done great things to me. His mercy goes on from generation to generation, to all who reverence him. How powerful is his mighty arm! How he scatters the proud and haughty

ones! He has torn princes from their thrones and exalted the lowly. He has satisfied the hungry hearts and sent the rich away with empty hands.

—LUKE 1:49–53, TLB

Because God hand-picked a servant girl to give birth to a King, Mary is declaring how God has done great and mighty things for her. She proclaims that His mercy is on those who fear the Lord.

As I try to picture this young woman, my thoughts tell me she was vulnerable, humble and possibly a little afraid. If you were a young woman about to be married and discovered you were pregnant, then tried to convince people that you had conceived the child through the power of the Holy Spirit, I think you would be a basket case!

When Mary walked on this earth, women were generally poor, vulnerable and uneducated—all qualities of a broken, humble spirit. Mary's response was, "I am the Lord's servant, and I am willing to do whatever he wants. May everything you said come true" (Luke 1:38, TLB). God was asking her to serve Him, and she submitted willingly, yet there was a cost for it. A divine exchange took place between God and Mary. She had to lay down any pride she had and be willing to face people who accused her of becoming pregnant before marriage.

Mary had to face her family and peers and hope they believed her story of what had really happened. Meanwhile, Joseph quietly considered divorcing her. Mary was shamed and devastated until an angel showed up and convinced him of the truth.

Many of us are like Mary—broken, humbled, and therefore usable by God. Mary's submission led to our salvation. She gave birth to King Jesus, who willingly paid the ultimate price for all our sins and shame. Her exchange with God brought us the most precious gift of life—Jesus, our Lord and Savior.

I am so glad she was a usable vessel. Are you at the same place with the Lord? Are you willing to be broken and humbled and to declare, "I am willing, Lord"? Are you willing to pay any price and be vulnerable as Mary was?

His Word shares how the Lord scatters the proud and the haughty ones, how He has torn princes from their thrones and exalted the lowly. As we look across our world, is this very thing not happening right before our eyes? We used to be a nation—a people—who stood for righteousness, and now every foundation of our nation is being shaken.

I think all of us need to be shaken, as Haggai 2:6–8 says: "For the Lord of Hosts says, 'In just a little while I will begin to shake the heavens and earth—and the oceans, too, and the dry land—I will shake all nations, and the Desire of All Nations shall come to this Temple and I will fill this place with my glory,' says the Lord of Hosts. The future splendor of this Temple will be greater than the splendor of the first one!" (TLB).

God wants His Temple rebuilt, and he has all the resources available to do it. God chooses to do His work through people, and all He needs are willing hands. Are you ready and available to do the work God is calling you to do? Are you willing to get your hands dirty for God?

First, we need to look deep within the core of our being and ask God to search our heart for any areas in need of deep repentance. Do you have places in your heart and life where you are proud and haughty? Do you need to re-evaluate your priorities? Are you open and ready to say, "I'm willing, Lord. I'll do it"?

For revival to come in our lives, there must be a time of repentance of sin and a returning to our first love. *Revival* means new life, rebirth, refreshment, renewal and restoration. Revival can be likened to the birthing process.

When a mother is pregnant, she must go through nine months of growth and waiting to be able to give birth to a precious child. Sometime during these nine months there is nausea, growth, aches and pains, weight gain, stretch marks, fatigue and more undesirable effects. But all of this must take place before a child can become big enough to be born. When a mother goes into labor she experiences intense pain, but by this time a mother will do just about anything to get this child out. She is tired of carrying her baby and ready and willing to give birth.

When those first pains occur mothers are sometimes not sure they can endure all the pain necessary to birth a child, especially when it's time to push. They are tired, they want to give up, and they don't think they have the strength to push. Then the baby's head is revealed, and the mother gets this elated feeling that a child is about to be born.

When a child is born, there is nothing in the world like it. An awesome miracle of God has just taken place. The entire room is filled with the incredible presence of the Lord, and all of heaven rejoices over this newborn who has taken his or her place in this world. Undeniable joy and newfound love fill the parents' hearts as they get their first glimpse of their newborn child. Time seems to stand still.

I remember when each of my three children were born. The awareness of God's awesome presence streaming through our hospital room was unbelievable.

As we laid our eyes on our newborn for the first time it was as if we already had a deep love for this child, and yet we didn't even know the baby personally.

I am sure God feels the same way about each one of us. When one of His children accepts Him as Lord of his life, God's response is overwhelmingly loving, and yet God already knew that individual before he was even a thought in his parents' minds. This is stated in Psalm 139:15–18, which says: "You were there while I was being formed in utter seclusion! You saw me before I was born and scheduled each day of my life before I began to breathe. Every day was recorded in your Book! How precious it is, Lord, to realize that you are thinking about me constantly! I cannot even count how many times a day your thoughts turn towards me. And when I waken in the morning, you are still thinking of me!" (TLB).

It is truly inspirational to understand and know that God loves us so much that He is constantly thinking about us—and was, even before we were born. Shouldn't we have enough time in our busy lives to spend some precious moments each day with the lover of our souls?

As God finished what He started with our birth, he will continue to do so in our lives.

Isaiah 66:7–9 says: "Before [Zion] travailed, she gave birth; before her pain came upon her, she was delivered of a male child. Who has heard of such a thing? Who has seen such things? Shall a land be born in one day? Or shall a nation be brought forth in a moment? For as soon as Zion was in labor, she brought forth her children. Shall I bring to the [moment of] birth and not cause to bring forth? says the Lord. Shall I Who causes to bring forth shut the womb? says your God" (AMP).

Our God will finish what He has started in us and in the world. In the birthing process, the finished product is a beautiful, precious child. In the process of birthing revival across the nations of this world, God also will complete the work that he has begun in all of us. When a child begins to be born, you cannot and would not stop the birth pains. The same can be said of the cost and the pain of revival. God will do His part, and we must do ours. We must come before Him with a humble and broken heart and repent of our sins and stand in the gap for the sins of others.

Repentance, or coming clean before the Lord, needs to occur on a daily basis. None of us is exempt from sin, and all of us fall short of the glory of God. Our flesh and our Spirit go to war daily. Every single day, we must deny our flesh and pick up the cross and follow Jesus. If we don't, the flesh will win, and sin always occurs. The only way to conquer sin is to have a humble and contrite spirit. Then God can change people's hearts and restore their land (lives).

If we don't cry out to God for forgiveness and stand in the gap for the sins of this nation, who will? If we want to see our nation restored and standing for righteousness, then the people who know God must repent and take a stand for righteousness.

The birthing process comes with pain, but with pain comes great joy. God promises us in Isaiah 66:12–14 that prosperity shall overflow and that He will send it, that He will comfort us much like a little one is comforted when she nurses on her mother. Our hearts will rejoice, and vigorous health will be ours. The world will see the good hand of the Lord upon His people. God has a glorious future planned for His people who are willing to pay the price of repentance and prayer.

Revival comes also by the hand of judgment. When Jesus returns, He will return as our judge. Isaiah 66:15–16 says, "For see, the Lord will come with fire and with swift chariots of doom to pour out the fury of his anger and his hot rebuke with flames of fire. For the Lord will punish the world by fire and by his sword, and the slain of the Lord shall be many!" (AMP).

We do not want to be on the side of the unfaithful. We do not want to get caught sneaking behind the Lord's back and trying to cover up our sins. We cannot, anyway. He sees everything we think, say and do. (See Psalm 139.)

When we cloak sin, we are trying to cover the shame of it. The enemy wants us to hide it and cover it up and make everything look good on the outside. But God wants to shine His marvelous light on our sin and shame. He wants all of us to trade in our sin and shame for His glory. We need to make this great exchange. He wants all of us to be free from the chains of shame. God wants every one of us to walk in the light of His Glory and make it to our final destiny—eternity with Him in heaven.

He is the One who gives us life, and He is the One for Whom we should live our lives.

A youth pastor gave me a saying that I will never forget. This saying still hangs on my wall: "What you are is God's gift to you. What you make of yourself is your gift to God." I want to be all that God wants me to be. I want to reflect His glory to this broken, dying world. I want to run the race that He has called me to run so I can share in His glory.

He has a place waiting for you and me. He has a new

name for each of us—if we choose Him. Isaiah 66:22 says, "As surely as my new heavens and earth shall remain, so surely shall you always be my people, with a name that shall never disappear. All mankind shall come to worship me from week to week and month to month. And they shall go out and look at the dead bodies of those who have rebelled against me, for their worm shall never die; their fire shall not be quenched, and they shall be a disgusting sight to all mankind" (TLB).

We have been a foolish nation, and sometimes we are foolish people. We are much like the children of Israel. When they left Egypt, they went into the desert of testing, and it took forty years to get to the Promised Land. Many of us are not willing to lay down every part of our lives. If we continue to withhold areas from the Lord we will be tested or disciplined, and the longer we fight it, the longer we will stay in the desert.

God's temple in the Old Testament was a physical building. In the New Testament, we learn that we are His temple when He dwells within us. Therefore, our relationship with Him is made possible because we are His dwelling place. That relationship also must be rebuilt when we rebuild His temple. We must exchange our selfish attitudes and motives for a restored relationship with God. The majority of us take better care of our own homes than this special relationship. As we put our priorities in order, everything we do must be as an act of worship to God. Then we will see His glory, His blessings and His provision for our lives (Haggai 2:19).

To get to the Promised Land, we must repent, be obedient to the Lord, cry out in prayer for His mercy, and stand back and watch God send revival and heal our land.

Please take the time right now to pray this prayer with me:

Dear Jesus, It is my heart's cry to see revival come to my own life and to the lives of others. For Your presence to totally affect everything I do, I must come to You daily with a humble heart. Jesus, please forgive me for the times I have placed You anywhere but first in my life. I know there have been many occasions when I have placed people or things above You. I repent, and I ask for Your forgiveness. Please come into my life and help me place You as my top priority. I want to be a part of rebuilding Your temple and seeing Your glory touch heaven and earth. Send restoration, Lord! Send renewal, Lord! Send Revival!

EPILOGUE

Come Away With Me, My Beloved

The town harlot's fingers were dripping with myrrh, a sweet perfume. She had filled the flask overflowing with oil, and it was spilling out all over the place as she walked along. She wanted to make sure she had enough oil to do her job well. She knew in her heart what she desperately longed to do, yet she needed the courage to act. She had carried her sin and shame around for so long that they had become her constant companions, as in a bad relationship, stalking her day and night, even in her dreams.

But this day was different from all the rest. She knew that Jesus was dining at one of the Pharisees' houses, and if she timed it just right, she would go in, an uninvited guest, and throw herself at the feet of Jesus. She could only hope that at His feet, she would find peace for her tormented soul.

She stood at the door of the Pharisee's house, afraid to knock yet too timid to burst in. She paused for a second, then she opened the door carefully. As the people looked up at her, she didn't make eye contact with anyone but Jesus. He held her gaze with a warm embrace of His enduring love. He knew she was coming. He had been waiting for her all along. This divine appointment would change her destiny.

Her tears started flowing the moment she began pouring the precious oil over the feet of Jesus. This woman didn't spare just a few drops of oil. She poured out the entire jar. She gave it all in a public, passionate display of broken worship.

This expensive perfume represented a whole year's salary, and yet to her, it meant more than just money. It was representative of her shattered life. She felt broken beyond repair, but as she anointed the feet of Jesus, a sweet-smelling fragrance was released in the room because of her humble, broken, wounded spirit. (See Isaiah 66:1–2.) God cannot pass by a broken and contrite heart. The cries of a passionate worshiper arrest the very heart of God, and He will move heaven and earth to meet with you. (See Psalm 51:10–17.)

She could not hold back any longer. She kissed Jesus' feet and lavished them with her warm tears of unashamed love. In one moment of time, she not only met an earthly need by cleaning the feet of Jesus, but she also ministered extravagant love, deeply touching His heart and crowning Him King of glory. This is one of the greatest acts of humble worship mentioned in the Bible.

This woman knew no boundaries. She uncovered her hair and let it hang down and began to dry His feet with it. In those days a woman's hair represented her glory, for it covered her. But this woman had no dignity left. She risked it all for one divine encounter at the feet of Jesus. It was her only chance to make this shame exchange.

Time seemed to stand still as the presence of God filled the room. Here was a humble, broken vessel pouring out her heart, and God's glory landed itself right in the middle of their dinner party. Things always seem to go from ordinary to extraordinary when the glory of the Lord shows up. What an unpredictable time for a shame exchange. Here was a woman "Shattered by Shame" who was about to get "Crowned in Glory." What a name exchange!

Immediately, the Pharisee tried to recover some composure by clearing his throat, as if he could say anything that would break this exchange. He stood and responded, "If this man was the prophet I thought he was, he would have known what kind of woman this is who is falling all over him" (Luke 7:37, The Message). Disgust was dripping from this self-righteous man's lips. He was pious and proud, with steeled eyes, ready for Jesus to respond to these accusations.

Jesus turned to respond, but no words could truly express how He was feeling. With tears streaming down His cheeks, he brushed the hair back from this woman's face. He wanted to see who it was that so lovingly touched His heart.

Jesus sighed deeply and began to speak. "'Do you see this woman? I came to your home; you provided no water for my feet, but she rained tears on my feet and dried them with her hair. You gave me no greeting, but from the time I arrived she hasn't quit kissing my feet. You provided nothing for freshening up, but she has soothed my feet with perfume. Impressive, isn't it? She was forgiven many, many sins, and so she is very, very grateful. If the forgiveness is minimal, the gratitude is minimal.' Then He spoke to her: 'I forgive your sins.' That set the dinner guests talking behind His back: 'Who does he think he is, forgiving sins!' He ignored them and said to the woman, 'Your faith has saved you. Go in peace'" (Luke 7:44–50, The Message).

What a sweet, powerful encounter with the most high God. When this woman got up, I am sure she left her shame at His feet and walked out crowned in God's magnificent glory. I picture this woman beaming with splendor, twirling down the dusty streets, free from her sin and shame once and for all.

We all need a shame exchange like that one.

Many of us have carried the burden of our sin and shame with us most of our lives. In fact, some of us have an imaginary backpack filled with our past, and we have grown weary under the weight of it all. Just like this woman, we long for a divine appointment with God that would change our destiny forever. We're desperate for a shame exchange.

It is time to pour out your shame and lavish His feet with your tears. Even if you feel you have no dignity left, take a risk. Don't hold anything back, and worship the Lord, unashamed, maybe for the first time in your life.

God is waiting to receive our most intimate worship and adoration. We must quiet our hearts from all the noise and distractions of our lives. We must stop worrying about what others may be saying or thinking about us. We must stop looking and listening to the things of our past that so easily entangle us and keep us stuck somewhere in the pain of our shame.

When we do this our lives will go from ordinary to extraordinary. He will take our shattered lives and crown us with His glory. Now that is a great exchange.

Allow Jesus to take your face into His hands and wipe your tears away. Let His forgiveness overwhelm you like sweet myrrh coming straight from His throne. The blood of Jesus was shed to heal the brokenhearted, to set all captives free, to comfort all who mourn, and to give us beauty in exchange for ashes, joy instead of mourning and a garment of praise instead of the spirit of heaviness.

We will be renamed Oaks of Righteousness planted by God to display His glory. "Instead of shame and dishonor, you shall have a double portion of prosperity and everlasting joy. For I, the Lord, love justice; I hate robbery and wrong. I will faithfully reward my people for their suffering and make an everlasting covenant with them" (Isa. 61:7–8, TLB).

Isaiah 62:3–4 says: "You'll be a stunning crown in the palm of GOD's hand, a jeweled gold cup held high in the hand of your God. No more will anyone call you Rejected, and your country will no more be called Ruined" (The Message). We will be His delight, the bride of Christ.

As we make these shame exchanges, God will reveal a fresh part of His character to us. He wants to pull us close to His secret place. However, true, genuine worship can only happen when we lay aside every distraction, all our sin and shame, and focus our heart, soul and mind on the Lord.

If we wait on the Lord, He will renew our strength. Then we will mount up with wings like an eagle. We will walk and not grow weary. We will run and not faint. (See Isaiah 40:31.)

As we wait on the Lord, He is wooing us to come away

with him. The Lord wants to develop a new level of intimacy with His people. He wants us to know His heartbeat. He wants us to see things from His perspective. He wants this because His ways are higher than ours. His thoughts are deeper than ours. (See Isaiah 55:8–9.)

I want to leave you with a song that is dear to my heart. God breathed the words to this song into my spirit as He showed me what He really thinks about me. Let these words minister to your spirit as He calls you to "Come Away With Me."

Behold, winter is past
The rain is over and gone
The flowers appear on the earth
The time for singing has come
Let Me hear your voice
And shelter you in My secret place
Oh, I long for your embrace
Come away with Me

Come away with Me, My beloved
My heart yearns to be with thee
Rise up My love, My fair one
Come away with Me

You are a fountain spring
Welling up within Me
I found whom My soul adores
As you draw near to Me
I'll draw nearer still
For I long to see your face
Abide in Me, I pray
Come away with Me

—LAURIE SMUCKER (1999)